D0903936

AMAZING STORIES

# TOM THOMSON

# TOM THOMSON

## The Life and Mysterious Death of the Famous Canadian Painter

HISTORY/BIOGRAPHY

by Jim Poling Sr.

PUBLISHED BY ALTITUDE PUBLISHING CANADA LTD.
1500 Railway Avenue, Canmore, Alberta T1W 1P6
www.altitudepublishing.com
1-800-957-6888

| | |
|---|---|
| Publisher | Stephen Hutchings |
| Associate Publisher | Kara Turner |
| Editor | Jay Winans |
| Digital Photo Colouring | Scott Manktelow |

We acknowledge the financial support of the Government
of Canada through the Book Publishing Industry Development
Program (BPIDP) for our publishing activities.

**Altitude GreenTree Program**
Altitude Publishing will plant twice as many trees as were used
in the manufacturing of this product.

**National Library of Canada Cataloguing in Publication Data**

Poling, Jim (Jim R.)
Tom Thomson / Jim Poling Sr.

(Amazing stories)
Includes bibliographical references.
ISBN 1-55153-950-0

1. Thomson, Tom, 1817-1917.  2. Painters--Canada--Bibliography.
I. Title.  II. Series: Amazing stories  (Canmore, Alta.)

ND249.T5P64 2003          759.11          C2003-904881-0

An application for the trademark for Amazing Stories™
has been made and the registered trademark is pending.

Printed and bound in Canada by Friesens
2  4  6  8  9  7  5  3

Cover: Tom Thomson as a young man

# Central Figures in the Tom Thomson Mystery

**The Artists**
Tom Thomson, Canadian landscape painter
J. E. H. MacDonald, painter and Thomson friend
A. Y. Jackson and others who would form the Group of Seven
Dr. James MacCallum, outdoorsman and patron of artists
George Thomson, Tom's brother and professional artist

**Canoe Lake People**
G. W. Bartlett, Algonquin Park superintendent
Mark Robinson, Algonquin Park ranger
Hugh Trainor, lumber company foreman
Winnie Trainor, Thomson's love interest
Shannon and Annie Fraser, operators of Mowat Lodge
The Bletchers, summer residents from Buffalo, N.Y.
George Rowe and Larry Dickson, guides
Jimmy Stringer, resident

**Medical People and Undertakers**
Dr. G. W. Howland, vacationer
Dr. A. E. Ranney, coroner, North Bay
F. W. Churchill, undertaker, Huntsville
M. R. Dixon, embalmer, Sprucedale
R. H. Flavelle, undertaker, Kearney

**The Grave Diggers**
William T. Little, park visitor
Leonard Gibson, Canoe Lake area resident
W. J. Eastaugh, park visitor
Frank Braught, cottager
Dr. Harry Ebbs, cottager

**The Investigators**
Dr. Noble Sharpe, head Ontario crime laboratory
Corporal A. E. Rodger, Ontario Provincial Police

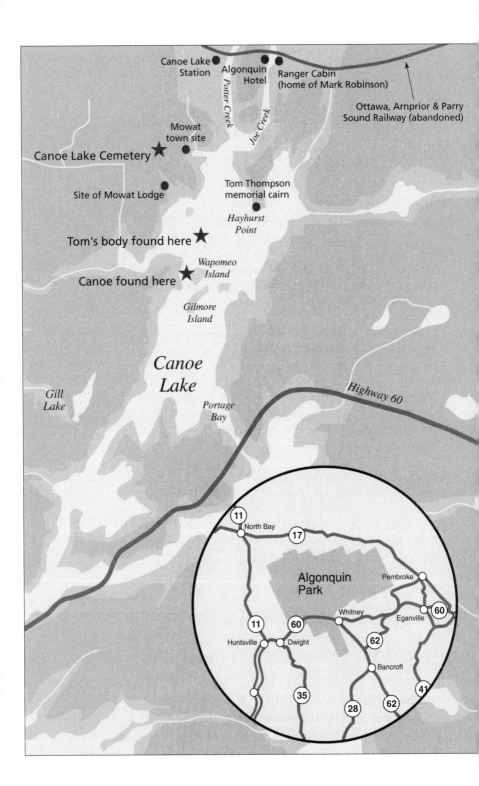

# Contents

# Prologue

*The Ojibwa called them* jiibyag — *the ghosts.*

*Their voices ride the night mists that slide quietly over the dark waters of Canoe Lake after the sun falls below the pines. They are most often heard off the three bigger islands — Wapomeo, Gilmour, and Cook — those sentinels that squat at mid lake as if to block access to the secrets that lie beyond. They whisper of amazing events that occurred here long ago.*

*Sometimes the mist carries more than the voices. On some summer nights, it is said, a dove grey canoe emerges from the north bay and slides southward, seemingly riding the mist itself and not the water. In it sits a man in a tan bush shirt and holding a paddle. He waves, then disappears.*

*The mist drifts to the western shore, then up the hillside overlooking the lake where a tiny graveyard struggles for its own existence against a relentless Mother Nature. Decaying picket fences and two tombstones gnawed by 10 decades of weather mark the graves of the two bodies officially buried there. One is a young man who died May*

*25, 1897, in a lumber mill accident. The other is a boy taken by a diphtheria epidemic at the lake.*

*But there is a third occupant there. And therein lies a mystery. A mystery wrapped in mysteries that no one can ever explain completely.*

*No one but the* jiibyag.

# Chapter 1
# Georgian Bay

neven rows of tombstones stand stiffly alert in the grassy clearing behind the red brick church that is as rugged and austere as the Presbyterian farmers who built it 140 years ago.

Some are high and handsome marble obelisks, others just homely stubs of white and grey stone. A few reflect the polish of newness; others are weather scoured and crusted with lichens, their names and dates approaching obliteration.

Each has a story to tell about people who lived and died in the rocky farm country of West Central Ontario.

None is as fascinating as the unpretentious grey granite stone 25 paces behind the magnificent oak shading the entire front half of the Leith United Church yard. The letters carved into the tombstone's polished face are small and simple and read:

Tom Thomson
Landscape Painter
Drowned Canoe Lake
July 8, 1917 Aged 39 years
11 months 3 days

Every visitor who stands before this gravestone surely asks the question: Does the coffin below really hold Tom Thomson's remains?

The tombstone is stubbornly silent. A shiver runs across the visitor's shoulders. Perhaps it's the chill brought by the icy breeze coming off the late spring ice pack still choking the long passageway that brings Georgian Bay to Owen Sound, the port city just a few kilometres south. More likely it's the thought that perhaps the coffin is vacant, its designated occupant maybe in another grave overlooking Canoe Lake in Algonquin Park 200 kilometres to the northeast.

Hundreds of Thomson pilgrims come here every year, all with the same question. They pass through the

Tom Thomson's tombstone

low gate on the wrought-iron fence separating the churchyard from the county road that runs past Rose Hill Farm where Thomson spent his boyhood. They leave without answers to the mystery of his death and hasty burial. Some people believe Thomson, just beginning to achieve success as an artist, was murdered at Canoe Lake.

Attempts to sort out the mysterious events of July 1917 always seem to leave them more tangled than before. Individual writers have tried. So have the Ontario government and powerful media, like the CBC. Still, after more than 85 years, the truth of what happened is not known and might never be.

## The Beginnings

The Tom Thomson story began in October 1877 when John and Margaret Thomson arrived to farm at the hamlet of Leith. They had lived comfortably enough at John's father's farm at Claremont, northeast of Toronto, where Thomas John Thomson, the sixth of ten children, was born August 5, 1877.

However, John had a vision of a new life on a farm up in Grey County. When his parents passed on, John Thomson set off in horse and buggy and explored farming country near Georgian Bay. He found a 14-room red brick house on a 40-hectare hillside not far off the bay. It was called Rose Hill and he bought it for $6600. He moved his family there in October 1877, when Tom was just two months old.

The family settled in well at the new farm. Tom was the third of five brothers — George, Fraser, Ralph, and Henry. A sixth died at birth. His sisters were Elizabeth, Louise, Minnie, and Margaret.

Thomson grew up a country boy, rambling through the fields and cedar and hardwood bushes of the land that slopes into Georgian Bay. He hunted in the woods and fished the streams, exhibiting few clues that he would become one of Canada's most famous artists. He did sketch caricatures in the hymnals at the red brick church. What child has not sought diversion from long and windy sermons?

He was sometimes seen as a bit different. He came by that naturally; his father was known in Leith as an eccentric who liked to stand in the fields and stare into the sky.

Tom had a rebellious side and was reported to have had problems with the minister at the church across the road. One time he received a dressing down for arriving for services in work clothes and stormed away angry with the minister.

Pursuit of fine art and other cultural activities were not a priority in Grey County in Thomson's boyhood. The area was typical Canadian bush country being tamed by settlers who came to exploit its natural resources. Snuggled beside Georgian Bay at the base of the wild Bruce Peninsula, the people of the Owen Sound area ran sawmills and gristmills, made furniture from the local hardwoods, raised sheep, and grew their famous Georgian Bay apples on the hillsides overlooking the bay.

Thomson grew up in an outdoor setting, learning the woodsman skills that he would need later for his trips into Algonquin Park. Much of what has been written about him has created the myth of a legendary woodsman. History has made him an expert canoeist and bush survivalist. Exaggerations of his outdoor skills have included references to his "Nativeness." He was well proportioned and athletic, grew to almost six feet tall and had dark looks, but Thomson was far from being Native in blood or bush skills. His level of bushcraft was that of the average farm boy of the day. He knew how to find himself around the woods and to keep himself warm and dry. Nothing in his upbringing around Leith would have qualified him for the voyageur status that some histories have given him. For instance, he was not a lifelong canoeist. The Thomsons always used boats, not canoes, when bringing in the winter supply of fish from Georgian Bay.

He did possess one exceptional outdoor skill — he was an expert angler. He loved fishing and studied it and became very good at it while still a child. His sister

Minnie remembered him as a small boy catching fish in the creek, cleaning them, and smoking them in a length of stovepipe. He read Izaac Walton, the Godfather of angling, and fished whenever he found the time and place. He was fishing when he died.

Life at Rose Hill was surely a country life, but not totally without cultural pursuits. Mrs. Thomson kept a decent library at home and the parents and children were considered well read. The Thomsons were a musical family. Tom sang in the choir and played the mandolin. He sometimes played drums with his brothers in the Leith hamlet band.

Four of the children — George, Tom, Margaret, and Fraser — took up painting, with George and Tom making a living from it. George lived a long life and achieved considerable success. His work has been exhibited from time to time with that of his famous brother.

Thomson passed elementary school at the one-room schoolhouse near Leith, and got at least partway through high school, leaving at 17. Nothing is known of his late teenage life, but no doubt he helped on the farm and pursued his love of the outdoors.

His adult life began to take shape at age 21 when he inherited $2000 from his grandfather. That was a lot of money in 1898 and relieved the usual pressure most young men felt to find a job.

## Tom Thomson

Tom tried to enlist as a soldier for the Boer War but was found unfit apparently because of flat feet. He then signed as an apprentice machinist in 1899 at the William Kennedy foundry in Owen Sound. He quit after eight months because he couldn't get along with the foreman. Not getting along with people he didn't like would become a recurring theme in his life.

The two oldest Thomson boys, George and Henry, left the farm to enroll in Canada Business College in Chatham, Ontario. After quitting the foundry, Tom followed them there to train for a white-collar office job. It is not known if he finished the course, but in 1901 he was out of there and onto unknown pursuits in Winnipeg, then Seattle where George had become an associate proprietor of the Acme Business College.

Tom enrolled in penmanship at Acme but quit to work at drawing for Maring and Ladd, a photoengraving company that did colour advertising. He moved over to competing Seattle Engraving Company, which paid him more money, and he became known as a fast and smart illustrator.

Three years in Seattle developed Thomson as an adult. He became a competent commercial artist and dabbled at drawing non-work-related sketches and watercolours. One piece that survived from those years is a self-portrait done in 1903. Thomson painted himself with his head tilted down and his eyes closed. It is a drawing of a reflective, perhaps even brooding, character. It strengthens the view of some Thomson followers that he was an erratic loner.

Some time after he made that self-portrait he fell in love with Alice Lambert, teenaged daughter of a minister. She was only 15 and highly strung and he was 27. He was smitten enough to blurt out a proposal of marriage. The outcome was disastrous; the young lady laughed at him, apparently out of nervousness. He took it as an absolute rebuff and left Seattle suddenly, some reports said the next day.

The shattered romance changed the direction of his life. Had young Alice accepted the proposal, Thomson likely would have remained on the West Coast, never to see the Algonquin Park wilderness that he would paint later with such power and colour.

That was 1904, and he returned to Leith to reconsider his life. He had much to think about. He had tried some work he didn't like, the Army had rejected him, and so had his first serious love. He had found work and some pleasure in drawing but had produced no art of any consequence.

There is no record of what he did when he retreated to the countryside of his youth. Again, he likely helped on the farm, hiked the bush, and most certainly pursued his passion — fishing. Whatever he did, he regrouped his thoughts, organized a plan, and headed south to Toronto to make a career as a commercial artist.

He was a country boy at heart but had tasted the urban life in Winnipeg and Seattle. He knew what Toronto had to offer and he had to try it, even though he would sacrifice his outdoor life.

Later, the highlights of big city life would fade and he would find himself back north. Not just for family visits in the Owen Sound area, but to the wilderness of Algonquin Park and his date with destiny.

# Chapter 2
# Toronto

oronto had split its backwoods cocoon wide open and was emerging as a major metropolitan centre when Tom Thomson, unemployed commercial artist, arrived from Grey County.

A booming economy drew in tens of thousands of immigrants who created ethnic enclaves that in turn made the boom echo. At the turn of the new century there were roughly 200,000 people in Toronto and that number doubled from the time of Thomson's arrival until the year of his death.

Construction chaos and human hustle greeted him

when he arrived at the downtown rail terminal. The Great Fire of 1904 had wiped out five-plus hectares of the commercial core. Rebuilding was frantic, with construction starts jumping 448 percent in 1905. New buildings were being erected everywhere, and all in brick and stone as a lesson learned from the devastating fire. The grand horticultural building at the CNE, Union Station, and Casa Loma, the castle home of financier Sir Henry Pellatt, all were built during Thomson's Toronto time.

There was a feast of activities in the big city. Toronto, as well as having rough slums, was developing an intellectual and cultural community. Art was coming into vogue and there were libraries and clubs and sporting events and elegant restaurants.

Thomson, despite being a loner, made friends who introduced him to the attractions of big city life. More importantly Toronto offered what Thomson had been seeking — a purpose in life. The boom times created good jobs in the commercial art field — jobs that offered a chance to develop and to meet people who shared enthusiasm for art.

He emerged in 1905 as senior illustrator for Legg Brothers, a commercial art firm that paid him $11 a week. He did design and lettering but quit suddenly over disagreements with the owners and moved on to

Grip Limited and later Rous and Mann, companies doing similar work in Toronto. These companies did a lot of general artwork, including design layouts for large stores.

The young man who had wandered somewhat aimlessly now had a life track to follow. His work brought satisfaction and the opportunity to develop. It also provided him friendship among colleagues and opportunities to discuss art with other people. His new friends encouraged him to paint, and at one point he took painting lessons.

One friend that he made at Grip was J. E. H. MacDonald, who was a few years older than Thomson and had trained as an artist. He urged Thomson and others to develop as landscape painters.

MacDonald was a stalwart of the Arts and Letters Club, formed in 1908 as a gathering spot for men interested in the arts. He introduced Thomson to the club, where men gathered for lunches, dinners, lectures, readings, pre-theatre drinks, and conversation. The club was the setting for Thomson's first exhibition, in 1911.

Meeting MacDonald and other artists changed Thomson's life. He didn't know it but he and the people he met would create a historic movement in Canadian art. He worked with Arthur Lismer, Fred Varley, Franklin Carmichael, Franz Johnson, and later Lawren Harris and A. Y. Jackson. These men and MacDonald formed the famous Group of Seven artists after Thomson's death. The Group, inspired by Thomson's work, became the first Canadian national school of painting and shaped the way Canadians view their landscape.

Thomson and his new friends talked about art at work and went on weekend sketching trips outside Toronto. The city was still small enough that woods pushed up against the downtown area. They could hike into the upper reaches of the Don and Humber Rivers, relatively unpolluted streams in those days, and paint in a forest atmosphere. Or, they could travel farther north to Lake Scugog and Lake Simcoe country.

Thomson didn't even have to go beyond the city to find bushland recreation. There is one story of him snowshoeing up Rosedale ravine, now part of the city centre, late at night and returning home at dawn.

Such quirky behaviour built Thomson a reputation as being different and sometimes difficult. Friends commented on his moodiness. A colleague at Legg once described him as difficult and erratic. Another employer called him quarrelsome. A. Y. Jackson once said that Thomson had fits of unreasonable despondency.

"He was a creature of depression and ecstatic moments," Lismer said many years after Thomson's death.

Mark Robinson, the Algonquin Park ranger who became his friend, called him melancholy, sometimes appearing "defeated in manner."

"He was a rather moody, quiet chap, and rather withdrawn," recalled Daphne Crombie, who got to know Thomson while nursing her husband back to health in Algonquin Park.

These observations helped create an impression of a split personality, or at least a man with two very different sides.

One side of Tom Thomson was the bon vivant. He dressed stylishly and enjoyed good restaurants. He wore silk shirts. He loved women and liked booze and drank heavily at times. He had money — initially from his inheritance, then the good wage of a commercial artist. At Rous and Mann he earned 75 cents an hour for a 46.5-hour week, a very decent wage for the times. He spent it with style and was generous and gregarious at times.

Contrast that with the brooding and socially monastic Thomson who wore bush trousers and a heavy work shirt and who preferred to sit smoking his pipe in the woods, staring blankly at the sky or water. He also had a violent temper, witnessed by a friend who watched him throw his sketch box into the woods in a fit of frustration. There are other stories of him storming from church because he didn't like the preaching and of tearing up a cheque in a fit of unreasonableness.

Which was the real Tom Thomson? A sunny new-century artist eating the best fare offered at the Arts and Letters Club in what was then the country's second largest city? Or the brooding woodsman dressed in fishing clothes and boiling water on the portage to Tea Lake?

He was probably both. Most of us have two different sides, and Thomson's are exaggerated by the exasperation of people who want to know more about him but can't because his time in the spotlight was so brief and so long ago.

Thomson adopted Toronto life and slid smoothly into its pace. If he ever found the urban setting oppressive, he could escape on day trips and holiday excursions back to the family farm.

After his 1905 arrival the city became his permanent home until 1913 when he began living the non-winter months in Algonquin Park. He stayed in rooming houses in Toronto, chiefly the home of Joseph Watson on Elm Street. He had a third-floor room and sometimes joined other boarders for evenings of chat in the downstairs living room but was known to say little.

The attachment to urban life loosened following a holiday outing in the spring of 1912. Thomson had a friend, Dr. J. M. McRuer, living in Huntsville, the lumber town just west of Algonquin Park, and knew a bit about the area from visiting him. Also he had heard other artists talk about the sketching opportunities offered by Algonquin. So he and friend H. B. (Ben) Jackson (no relation to A. Y. Jackson) went into Algonquin for two weeks. They set up a tent at the Tea Lake Dam and spent their time exploring, sketching, and, of course, fishing.

Jackson described his friend on that trip:

"Tom was never understood by lots of people, was very quiet, modest. He cared nothing for social life, but with one or two companions on a sketching and fishing trip, with his pipe and Hudson Bay Tobacco going, was a delightful companion. If a party or the boys got a little loud or rough Tom would get his sketching kit and wander off alone. At times he liked to be that way. Wanted to be by himself."

**Two Legends Meet**

The trip must have honed Thomson's hunger for a bigger bite of the outdoors. Late in July 1912 he embarked with friend Bill Broadhead for the woodlands northwest of Sudbury. They canoed the Mississagi and Spanish Rivers, ending up on the North Channel of Lake Huron in late September.

The adventure lasted two months and anyone having illusions about Thomson being a master canoeist at that point should note they capsized at least twice during the trip. They lost sketches and dozens of rolls of photographic film in the dumpings. Despite the loss, Thomson described the trip as a great adventure through the world's best canoe country.

The trip produced another Tom Thomson legend, a meeting with Archie Belaney, the man later known as Grey Owl. Various stories have them meeting briefly in the Mississagi Forest Reserve and Grey Owl later visiting Thomson's Toronto studio.

The Mississagi meeting is plausible, if only because Belaney was in the area at the same time. He arrived in Biscotasing on the Canadian Pacific Railway in 1912 and became well known for being drunk and disorderly. Biscotasing would have been the jumping-off spot for Thomson and Broadhead to begin their summer-long canoe trip.

There is no definitive proof of the meeting, and it is possible Belaney made it up. He was a champion teller of tall tales, the biggest one being the story of his own identity.

He said he was born in Mexico to an Apache mother and a Scot father who was a Native scout. He drifted north and lived among the Ojibwa of the Temagami region, learning northern woods skills.

When Grey Owl died in 1938 at age 49, the *North*

*Bay Nugget* reported that he was a fraud. Grey Owl was a full-blooded English boy born in Hastings, England, and raised by his aunts. He ran away to Canada when he was 18 and became known as a bigamist and binge drinker, an emotionally damaged man who had been abandoned by a no-good father.

Still, the Grey Owl persona he cultivated became a mentoring symbol for a modern conservation movement. His writings, lectures, and work to preserve beaver populations were positive contributions that in the public's mind overrode his deceit.

Both Thomson and Grey Owl are seen to this day as reminders of the need to maintain a balance between civilization and nature. Whether they ever met and shook hands in the forests they both so obviously loved really doesn't matter.

There is, however, one proven tie between the two men. They both crossed the path of Mark Robinson, legendary Algonquin Park ranger. Robinson and Thomson became friends later, but Belaney met the ranger in unfriendly circumstances.

Poaching was rampant in North America, including Algonquin Park, early in the 20th century. In 1908 an investigation was ordered to bear down on poaching in the park. Belaney knew the difficulties rangers had nabbing poachers, and being a boastful man, broadcast to friends that he was smart enough to outwit any ranger in Algonquin Park. He bet someone that he could cross the park from one side to another in winter without being caught.

Somehow park officials heard of the bet. When Belaney entered the park along the logging road from Dorset on Lake of Bays, ranger Bud Callighen cut his tracks and caught up with him. However, Belaney took off again, trying to outrun the ranger. At Ragged Lake he fell through the ice on a beaver pond and lost his pack containing his survival gear, including matches. When Callighen found him he had frozen feet.

Callighen brought Belaney to Canoe Lake where Robinson nursed him to health and sent him packing when he was able to travel.

Thomson was living in Toronto at the time. Several years would pass before he joined Grey Owl and Robinson among the ranks of bush legends.

When he was introduced to the northern forests during the 1912 Algonquin and Mississagi canoe treks, the experiences tipped the balance between his city and country lives. After the winter of 1912–1913, Thomson headed north again to Algonquin and would seldom be seen again in Toronto when the snow was not on the ground.

# Chapter 3
# Algonquin Park

hen Tom Thomson walked across the Canoe Lake rail station platform in May 1913 he entered a world light years away from Toronto.

The station itself was quite civilized looking for a backwoods stop. It was a two-storey building and oddly shaped because the second floor was built at right angles to the first, creating four peaks and platform overhangs. Its white clapboard siding was somewhat greyed by years of northern weather, but the large black letters spelling CANOE LAKE on each end of the building were still prominent.

Crowding the station were thousands of kilometres of bush country consisting of pre-Cambrian rock, hardwood hills, spruce bogs, and myriad lakes and rivers that seldom felt a human presence. It had been protected for 20 years as Algonquin Park, and, as Thomson arrived, it was undergoing a remarkable transition.

The 7700-square-kilometre Algonquin preserve was changing from a natural resources factory to a recreation and relaxation environment. From the early 1830s it had been logged brutally for its ancient white and red pines that brought top dollars in Europe's shipbuilding markets. Now it was on the verge of becoming a playground in a newly developing tourism industry.

It was ideally located, running the southern edge of the Canadian Shield between Georgian Bay and the Ottawa River Valley, and no more than 250 kilometres north of the southern Ontario population centres. It was within a day's journey from the city lights, but still relatively remote and wild.

Algonquin, set aside as a wildlife sanctuary in 1893 by the Ontario legislature, was the product of a late-1880s change in society throughout North America. Canadians and Americans had adopted an industrial life in the cities. Conservation movements arose to change the attitude that forests and their wildlife were forever no matter how they were managed. With the conservation movements came an outdoor health craze based on the premise that the northern woods invigorated the body, mind, and soul.

Travel brochures broadcast the healthy wonders of the great North Country. Grand Trunk Railways System, which had a line through the park, trumpeted itself as the "Highway to Health."

G. W. Bartlett, an early Algonquin superintendent, joined the promotion by championing the park as a safe place to holiday, with a nod to the government's wolf extermination policy. Conservation movements had done nothing to eliminate man's pathological fear and hatred of wolves, which Bartlett referred to as "brutes." People didn't want to go north for health only to be eaten by wolves, and Bartlett and his people assured their safety by shooting, trapping, and poisoning every wolf they could find.

Taking to the outdoors for improved mental and physical health became trendy. Doctors recommended northern vacations, or even moving north for healthier living.

Figures who later featured prominently in the Tom Thomson mystery chose northern living for its beneficial air. Mark Robinson went to the park as a ranger in 1907 because he had been seriously ill and his doctor advised him to find healthy outdoor work up north.

Doctors themselves accepted the call north for health as much as others. American Dr. R. P. Little, who knew Thomson well, was an early park summer resident who cited health as a reason for being there.

Cottages appeared, either as new construction or renovation of buildings abandoned in the fading lumber trade. Lodges opened to accommodate the increasing flow of visitors. Highland Inn, the Algonquin, Camp Mowat on Canoe Lake, Nominigan Lodge on Smoke Lake, and Minnesing on Island Lake became immediate attractions to city folk searching for healthy vacations. Summer camps for children followed.

**The Artists Arrive**

The park was a natural for anglers, campers, hikers, canoeists, and people who just wanted to lie around, feel the sun, and breath the fresh air. However, it also was discovered early by the artistic set. A group from the Toronto Art Students' League took a sketching trip to the park in 1902 and brought back enthusiastic reports of the scenery. Word spread and soon Algonquin was a priority location for sketching. Reports like these likely enticed Thomson to his first Algonquin visit in 1912.

The sight of painters in the woods mystified bush-hardened loggers who remained in the park. There is one story of a logger seeing Tom Thomson near Canoe

Lake and reporting: "He had three sticks stuck up and a bit of board, and he was dabbing paint on. I don't know what he was doing." When told the man was an artist, the logger just shook his head and said he'd never heard of such a thing.

Ralph Bice, the legendary Algonquin Park trapper and guide, was a teenager during Thomson's last years and once recalled how bush people regarded artists. "Artists then didn't have a very high rating ... unless you were out working doing something, why you weren't much thought of." Perhaps that's why Thomson worked part-time during most of his four-and-a-half Algonquin summers. Painting full time likely would have left him labelled a useless city slicker.

It is hard to imagine why the Canoe Lake scenery intrigued Thomson when he arrived in the spring of 1913. Canoe Lake is not the prettiest that Algonquin offers, and it was a lot less pretty 90 years ago.

It is a small to medium lake, covering roughly three-and-a-half square kilometres, including five or six significant bays that create prominent points of land. It is a rectangle, jagged on all shores, running almost four kilometres north to south. Its widest spot is not much more than one kilometre across.

There is a depressing lowland feel to it. Stretches of the shoreline are relatively flat and harbour lowland growers such as spruce, balsam, and hemlock. The first impression is not of the rolling and rocky highlands topography for which Algonquin is famous. You have to look beyond the north end of the lake to fully see sturdy hillsides rising into the hardwood forests whose autumn colours so fascinated Thomson and his contemporaries.

The northwest end is where all the action took place in Thomson's time. Canoe Lake Station was on Potter Creek roughly three kilometres north of the shrinking lumber village of Mowat. The creek drains south into the lake, and rail baggage could be shot down a chute from the station to a landing area. Boats or canoes then took it across the north end of the lake to Mowat.

Mowat was the first site for the Algonquin Park headquarters, but that was later moved to Cache Lake, likely because it was much more scenic. Canoe Lake might have returned to being just another quiet wilderness lake when the headquarters moved, but one of the most incredible business ventures in Canadian history assured the lake area its prominent place in Algonquin history.

In 1892, the year before the park was established, Gilmour and Co. of Trenton, bought the logging rights to almost 23,000 hectares of forest around Canoe and Tea Lakes. They decided to float the logs from Canoe Lake to sawmills at Trenton, more than 400 kilometres south. Engineers designed a colossal mechanical tramway to transport the logs over some high hills but the scheme was a complete disaster. The Gilmour Canoe Lake operations went bankrupt after creating the village of Mowat, which in 1896 had 700 people and 18 kilometres of rail sidings. The village was destined to return to the bush until the coming of health tourism saved at least part of it.

Shannon Fraser was appointed in 1907 to supervise the dismantling of the Canoe Lake lumbering operation. In 1913 he and his wife Annie, noting the trend to healthy outdoor recreation, took over a couple of Gilmour buildings and created Camp Mowat, which soon became Mowat Lodge.

Fraser, who always had a new scheme for promoting the lodge, bought a horse and coach that was used as a taxi service along the tote road from the station to Mowat. It's likely that Thomson, hauling camping gear and art supplies, took the coach from the station to Fraser's Mowat Lodge where he planned to stay.

What he saw on his arrival was the wreckage of the park's dying lumber industry. Mowat had emptied and was a network of little-used rail sidings, rundown sawmill works, horse barns, abandoned equipment and a treeless and bleak chip yard strewn with sawmill tailings. The mill yard mess covered more than 12 hectares.

In this setting sat the lodge, a whitewashed clapboard building of two storeys. It had been the lumber mill kitchen and boarding house and it overlooked the desolation of the millworks' ruins.

Beyond the industrial damage, however, were hundreds of square kilometres of relatively raw wildness. Thomson could pack his canoe with fishing and drawing equipment and paddle or portage into the best of Algonquin scenery in short order.

Thomson, like Algonquin, was undergoing a transformation when he arrived at Canoe Lake. He had just made his first serious sale: the Ontario government bought *A Northern Lake*, painted from his first trip to Algonquin the year before. It fetched $250, which represented two or three month's salary and boosted his decision to quit Rous and Mann. He was so thrilled with the sale that he took the full amount in one-dollar bills when he cashed the cheque and threw the handful of bills happily into the air, letting them settle down on him like large snowflakes.

The sale gave him more than money. It provided a much-needed shot of confidence. Thomson had only weak faith in his ability and placed little value on his paintings. The sale proved that his work did have value and marked the start of his life as a serious painter.

The money from *A Northern Lake* was significant but not enough to keep Thomson painting full time. However, his overhead was little — he stayed with the Frasers, or used a shack nearby, or tented, quite often across the lake at Hayhurst Point. He helped the Frasers, planting a garden and doing odd jobs, as they developed Mowat Lodge into a comfortable lodge with a veranda where guests could sit and enjoy the breeze off the lake. Dr. Little recalled that Thomson lived on fish, flapjacks, bacon, and potatoes.

Thomson certainly was not the starving and struggling artist that some romantics have painted him to be. He was casual with money, buying expensive pipes and tobacco and clothing. He used expensive paints. Once, he became angry in a bank and tore up a cheque when a teller refused to cash it unless someone attested to his identity.

He often gave his paintings away. Mark Robinson told *Maclean's* magazine in 1953 of the day he watched Thomson painting *The West Wind*, which has become one of the artist's most famous paintings. Robinson noted it was a wonderful painting, although still unfinished.

"If you like it that much," Thomson said, "you can have it."

"No, no you can't give that one away Tom," replied the ranger. "One of these days they'll see what you're doing and it will be worth a lot of money."

*The West Wind*, described by A. Y. Jackson as one of the three best Canadian paintings, now hangs in the Art Gallery of Ontario and would fetch hundreds of thousands of dollars if ever sold.

Despite his casualness about money, he did think about how he would support himself without full-time work. Or, perhaps he just wanted to work to be seen 'right' in the eyes of men like Ralph Bice.

In 1913 he did a bit of guiding, which paid four dollars a day for a main guide and two dollars for the secondary man. Fire rangering paid $2.50 a day, and he considered applying for one of those positions during his first year in the park. However, he felt that it was late in the season to apply and that he could make some money by finding work at a commercial art firm during the winter.

By summer's end he knew one thing for certain: he wanted to spend more time painting. He thought he could do that and earn some regular income by doing piecework as a commercial artist or by working part-time in the woods as a ranger and guide.

Any worries he had about money disappeared on his return to Toronto in October 1913. He visited J. E. H.

MacDonald in his studio and there met Dr. MacCallum, a professor of ophthalmology at the University of Toronto, outdoorsman, and patron of the arts. MacCallum got to know Thomson, was enthused about his work, and offered to pay his expenses for a year so he could paint full time. MacCallum later provided the money to convert a cabinetmaker's tool shed into a studio that became known as Thomson's Shack.

The shack, where Thomson spent his remaining winters, was behind the Studio Building at 25 Severn Street, just off Yonge Street and north of Davenport Road. MacCallum also helped finance construction of the Studio Building as a place where Toronto artists could work. It opened in January 1914, and Thomson shared studio space there for a while with A. Y. Jackson.

Tom Thomson was now a full-time artist with a sponsor. He painted all winter, gaining confidence with every piece. When the hot spring sun of 1914 began to melt the northern snows, he was free to follow his dream — paddling Algonquin Park with a fishing pole and sketchboards.

His dream of becoming an itinerant landscape painter set free in the wilderness was about to come true. But it would be a brief dream. Trouble was already beginning to ripple the calm of Canoe Lake.

# Chapter 4
# Tensions at Canoe Lake

By almost any account, the Bletcher family was not anyone's favourite neighbours on Canoe Lake. They owned one of the summer places clustered on the northwest shoreline. They were among the earliest summer residents, but of all the thousands of words written about incidents on the lake, none have ever been complimentary of the Bletchers.

They were known as a family with a stubborn streak, pleasant enough at times, but flinty and uncompromising at others.

Martin Bletcher Sr. was a German-American from Buffalo, New York, where he operated a furniture factory.

In 1905 he bought a vacant lumber mill house on the shores of Canoe Lake and turned it into a cottage. There he spent summer vacations with his wife, son Martin Jr., and daughter Bessie. The children were in their late teens or early twenties at Thomson's arrival in the park. Martin was a private investigator in Buffalo, and Bessie was a teacher and amateur artist. Martin is also said to have had a wife who was seen occasionally at the cottage.

When the First World War erupted in 1914, the Bletchers' Germanic background set them aside in the small summer community. Their loyalties were torn between the old country and the new one. Some folks felt the Bletchers were outright sympathetic to the German cause.

Perhaps the tensions of their ancestry playing against the background of the war prompted Mrs. Bletcher to react stubbornly to a silly incident in the summer of 1914. Ottelyn Addison recalled the incident in her book *Early Days in Algonquin Park*. Mrs. Addison was the daughter of Mark Robinson, the park ranger, and spent much of her life in and around Algonquin and collected park history.

That summer was Thomson's second full painting season at Canoe Lake. He was well known by everyone there and was considered part of the community, even though he often disappeared for long painting and fishing treks.

He was there the morning someone on the lake noted that the Bletchers were flying the Stars and Stripes by itself on their cottage flagpole. World convention allows flying of a foreign flag only if the flag of the site country is flown above it. Neither the Union Jack nor the Canadian Ensign flew at the Bletcher cottage.

It is possible that the Bletchers always had flown the American flag alone and that the Canadian nationalism brought out by going to war suddenly made people take close notice of it. The U.S. hadn't entered the war yet and maybe some people were upset about that.

Algonquin Park in those days was like a colony, governed by the park superintendent and his ranger staff. They had the power to make rules and enforce rules and kept busy fingers in day-to-day happenings.

So it was not unusual that Mark Robinson appeared at the Bletcher door that particular morning and informed Mrs. Bletcher that the flag could not be flown without the Union Jack or Ensign above it. He left expecting that the situation would be corrected.

The Bletchers did nothing. The American flag continued to fly alone. On two consecutive mornings they rose to find the flag rope cut and the Stars and Stripes lying in a heap. They dutifully repaired the rope and ran the flag up again.

Robinson appeared at the Bletcher cottage to complain once again about the breach of flag protocol. Mrs. Bletcher flew into a rage and chased him off the property with a broom.

Visitors at Mowat Lodge noticed that on the third morning Tom Thomson sat on the lodge veranda, studying the Bletcher place through field glasses. He was looking at the flagpole on which a small Union Jack flew above the Stars and Stripes. Thomson had been the one who cut the rope on two nights and hoisted the small Jack on the third.

The flag incident was seen as great fun, but it underlined a tension between the Bletchers and some lake inhabitants, notably Thomson. Robinson told his daughter later that there was ill will between Thomson and Martin Jr., but no reason was ever given for it.

Life returned to normal at Canoe Lake. Thomson pursued the life of a wandering woodsman-artist, travelling by canoe. Everything he needed was in his canoe, one of his most prized possessions. It was a wood strip and canvas Chestnut, built by the famous Chestnut Canoe Co. in Fredericton, New Brunswick. Thomson bought it in 1914 and painted it a distinctive dove grey, producing the colour by including an expensive tube of paint from his artist's supplies.

He covered huge distances in his canoe, paddling into the far reaches of the park and well beyond. One trip that summer of 1914 was to Dr. MacCallum's cottage on Go Home Bay in Georgian Bay. He painted through much of the summer there, enjoying the hospitality of his patron.

He paddled back to the park in September to entertain his artist friends from Toronto. Varley, Lismer, and A. Y. Jackson had taken up his invitation to come up the park to paint the electric fall colours.

Someone at Mowat Lodge recalled it was a happy time with the friends enjoying the outdoors and each other's company.

Lawren Harris described in a lecture many years later the atmosphere at such gatherings of the painter friends: "We lived in a continuous blaze of enthusiasm. We were at times very serious and concerned, at other times hilarious and carefree. Above all, we loved this country and loved exploring and painting it."

That atmosphere of pleasant comradeship would not be seen again at Canoe Lake.

After the gathering of painter friends, Thomson packed up his sketches and returned to Toronto for the winter. Late autumn often is depressing there, with grey skies, swirling snow, and the cold hints of weather that lies ahead.

# Tensions at Canoe Lake

The approaching winter of 1914–15 was especially depressing because of the war. Some of Thomson's friends, including A. Y. Jackson, answered the call for recruits and put their painting careers on hold. Thomson tried again to enlist but was rejected.

He spent another winter in Toronto painting from the sketches he had made. When he tired of painting he carved canoe paddles and axe handles and worked on designing his own fishing lures.

Snowbound and tethered to the city, Thomson ached to return north. However, when winter departed, making way for the spring and summer of 1915, life was different in the park. The war had slowed tourism and some of the main players had been packed off to the killing grounds of Europe.

Thomson arrived at the park early but stayed close to Mowat Lodge until July. Then he paddled away to paint furiously, reporting later to MacCallum that he had done 100 sketches. He also worked as a fire ranger.

The most notable incident on the lake that summer was a diphtheria outbreak that killed one of the Hayhurst children in July. The boy, eight-year-old Alexander, was buried at the Mowat cemetery, one of two recorded burials there, a fact that would be raised time and again later in the arguments over Tom Thomson's real resting place.

**Romance Creates More Tensions**
The following year, 1916, Thomson worked full time as a fire ranger and was posted to the northern section of the park. It was a hot, dry summer and active fire season, and he complained that rangering took away from his painting time.

It also took him away from something else — a love interest. It has never been recorded exactly when something sparked between Thomson and Winnifred Trainor, but certainly they had known each other at the lake for some time, possibly since 1913 when Thomson first took up annual summer residence.

The Trainors had a cottage fashioned from a cabin that had been a park substation, two doors over from the Bletchers. The father, Hugh, was a foreman for Huntsville Lumber Company, and he and his wife had two daughters, Winnifred, the eldest, and Marie. They spent summers at the lake and winters in a comfortable home in Huntsville.

Thomson visited Winnie at both places. He sometimes spent a couple days at the Huntsville home while coming and going to the park and used the cottage on occasion. He gave her gifts, including paintings.

There were rumours at the lake that Tom and Winnie were secretly engaged.

The fact that the Trainor and Bletcher cottages

were only two doors apart raised more speculation about the dislike that Thomson and Martin Bletcher Jr. had for each other. Some people suspected that Martin had eyes for Winnie and that Thomson was jealous of Bletcher's close proximity to her, especially so in 1916 while he was off in the woods fire rangering and painting. Whether there was any substance to that speculation will never be known now.

One of the difficulties in piecing together details of the Thomson-Winnie relationship is that Winnie did not talk much about herself or her times with Thomson.

The details of her life were lost in the shock and mystery of the Canoe Lake tragedy. She lived most of her life in Huntsville where she became a well-known eccentric. In fact, many people simply called her a crazy old lady. She never married and lived on the top floor of her parents' house where Thomson had visited. She rented out the main floor and would tell prospective renters that not many people could boast having a living room painted by the famous Tom Thomson.

She had 13 to 16 original paintings that Thomson gave her, and the rumour was that she kept them wrapped in newspapers and stored in a trunk at the house. She still went to the family cottage later and would appear occasionally at the Canoe Lake Cemetery.

Winnie told people throughout the years that she

and Thomson were engaged and planned to marry at the end of that tragic summer. Many people dismissed this because of her eccentricity.

Thomson himself left some evidence of the truth. He took a photo of Winnie on a fishing trip circa 1916, which means it also could have been the spring of 1917. The photo shows a tall woman in a chin-to-ankles gingham dress fitted at the waist. She is holding a string of fish and fishing rod. The fronts of the fingers gripping the rod are visible. On the lady's engagement/wedding ring finger is one, possibly two, rings. Friendship ring? Engagement ring?

Oddly, in the many thousands of pages printed about Tom Thomson over the decades nothing appears to have been written about the rings in that photo. Everything considered, it must be safe to assume that the ring or rings she wore were a link to the love she was about to lose forever.

# Chapter 5
# The Last Weekend

ife was simple and quiet at Canoe Lake in Tom Thomson's time. The frenetic distractions of today had yet to be discovered, and entertainment consisted mainly of evening gatherings for talk, or solitary reflection.

Sometimes people would take an evening paddle on the lake or stroll the little townsite. Mostly though, visitors sat out on the veranda of Mowat Lodge, watching the darkness consume the lake while discussing the latest news, most of it brought in by the railway. In poor weather they assembled in the living or dining areas.

After August 1914 the talk always centred on the

war in Europe. Britain had declared war on the German-Austrian-Italian alliance, and Canada, as a colony, entered it with enthusiasm. The war touched every Canadian. You couldn't escape it, even at remote Canoe Lake. In excess of 600,000 Canadians served, and 66,000, more than one in 10, never returned.

The war would have been a major topic of discussion on the evening of July 7, 1917, when a group of men gathered at the cabin of George Rowe, a popular fishing guide. Among those there were Thomson, lodge owner Shannon Fraser, and Martin Bletcher Jr.

Evening gatherings at the lake did not usually include alcohol. Temperance movements were on the march across Canada, and drinking was frowned upon in many circles. Besides, liquor was not always easy to come by in the bush.

But it was present at this particular Saturday night gathering. That's likely why the men were gathered without the women, out of sight, at Rowe's cabin. No one knows how much booze flowed, but there was enough to make several of the participants argumentative.

Tom Thomson became depressed whenever talk turned to the war. He could paddle a canoe hundreds of miles and portage it on his shoulders over rough terrain, but he wasn't deemed physically able to serve his country, like some of his friends. A. Y. Jackson had gone overseas. Mark Robinson had been over and just returned, wounded.

At that very time — July 1917 — another Owen Sound boy, William Avery (Billy) Bishop, was being adulated for his skills as an air ace and his stunning raid a month earlier on a German air base. Later that year Bishop would be the centre of a hero's homecoming celebration in Owen Sound.

So as the evening progressed with ugly war news mixed with alcohol, Thomson became even more depressed than usual.

Martin Bletcher Jr. was a loud and boastful man known to become even more obnoxious when he drank. As the party progressed he made comments about German superiority in the war.

His senses dulled by booze, Bletcher boasted that the Germans were winning. It was the wrong thing to do, at the wrong time. He ignored the sensitivity of the Canadians, who were losing friends and relatives to the war every day, while the Americans sat it out.

Thomson took offence to the boastful talk. He likely made reference to people like A. Y. Jackson and Robinson, now limping from a wound taken at Vimy, while Bletcher lounged part of the summer at Canoe Lake.

Some versions of the drinking party have Thomson

accusing Bletcher of being a draft dodger. That is unlikely because the U.S. did not fully enter the war until later that year. Bletcher did in fact become a suspected dodger later. He registered for the draft as required late in 1917, but when he was called up in 1918, he failed to report. However, the U.S. government investigated and ruled his failure to report had not been intentional and honourably discharged him.

Whatever was said ignited an intense argument. Before the night was over, some guides had to separate the two as they started to engage in a fistfight.

Bletcher left the party about midnight, hurling at Thomson words that would be recalled for decades: "Don't get in my way if you know what's good for you!"

There also were reports of other tousles that evening, including one between Thomson and Fraser over money. It appears to have been one of those nights in which liquor loosened tongues and attitudes and sparked rowdy drunken arguing.

There was some rough talk and pushing, but no blood was spilled, and late into the night everyone was safely in bed sleeping off the liquor.

**Sunday, July 8, 1917**
Dawn arrived with depressingly grey drizzle. The community at the northwest end of Canoe Lake stirred to life

slowly, the partygoers no doubt trying to shake off hangovers from the night before.

Thomson rose early, trout on his mind. He walked with Shannon Fraser up to the dam that controlled the water emptying in the northeast arm of Canoe Lake from Joe Lake. Thomson caught a big trout but lost it and went to the Algonquin Hotel on Joe Lake for late breakfast. He lingered with some of the guests, smoking and drinking coffee or tea.

About noon, he gathered his stuff for an afternoon trip down Canoe Lake where he could fish at Gill Lake or Tea Lake Dam. He loaded in his canoe some bread and bacon and a rubber ground sheet, plus his fishing tackle. He was off by early afternoon. Fraser reported seeing him paddling away and letting out his copper trolling line as he went. The canoe disappeared behind Little Wapomeo Island as it made its way south. That is the last time Tom Thomson was seen alive.

Some writers of the Thomson tragedy have said that only one person — Shannon Fraser — actually saw the artist that morning. They use this to argue that in fact Thomson was not seen that morning and was already dead.

A couple hours after Thomson left, Martin and Bessie Bletcher were on the lake in a boat with a small outboard motor. They spotted an overturned canoe.

Oddly, they did not investigate but carried on their way down the lake. On their way back they did not see the canoe, which apparently had drifted off.

Another version of the story has Bletcher towing the canoe to his boathouse but not telling anyone until the next day.

People at the lake later had much to say about that. It was considered unusual that someone would not investigate an overturned canoe. Also, people thought the Bletchers should have recognized the dove grey canoe as Thomson's.

### July 9 to July 16, 1917

Martin Jr. was at Mowat Lodge the next morning, Monday, the 9th, and mentioned seeing a canoe the afternoon before. Someone went out to find the canoe and brought it in. They reported to Mark Robinson that it was Thomson's. He called the park superintendent, who told him to start searching for the painter, now presumed missing.

A search was mounted. The bush on the south and west areas of the lake was scoured without finding a sign. The assumption was that Thomson's canoe must have slipped its mooring while he was in the bush, or that it had tipped him and he had swam to shore. Mark Robinson said search time was better spent looking for an injured Thomson in the woods than dragging the lake for a body.

Thomson was known to be a good canoeist and strong swimmer. Everyone seemed to dismiss the possibility that he could drown, and so the search of the shores continued day after day. Gunshots were fired and whistles blown, but there was not a trace of Thomson. The lake was not dragged.

George Thomson, Tom's older brother, arrived from New Haven, Connecticut, on Thursday, July 12. He talked with people on the lake about what could have happened and left a day or two later to comfort his aging parents in Owen Sound.

It was miserable searching. It rained almost every day during the week and mornings were cool. Robinson was exhausted and on Saturday, almost a week after Thomson disappeared, took a day off.

He resumed searching Sunday and planned to go out again Monday morning. Before he could leave, Charlie Scrim, fishing guide and friend of Tom's, came to his door. Charlie had tears on his cheeks.

"Mark, they've found Tom's body," Charlie is reported to have blurted out.

Dr. G. W. Howland, a vacationer from Toronto, had spotted the body in the lake.

An overturned canoe. A body recovered. Presumably

## *Tom Thomson*

Thomson drowned. That should have been the end of it. It was only the beginning.

# Chapter 6
# A Body
# Twice Buried

r. Howland was relaxing at a rented cottage on Little Wapomeo Island when he noticed some unusual flotsam in the lake. He couldn't tell immediately what it was, but he also saw a canoe carrying two people drifting by. He hollered, and the canoe, paddled by George Rowe and fellow guide Larry Dickson, held up.

Howland, a doctor and professor of neurology at the University of Toronto, yelled to the men to investigate. They paddled closer to the object, which looked like an animal carcass, perhaps a large loon.

"It's the body of man," one of the guides yelled back.

That was quickly followed by "It's Tom Thomson!"

The guides towed the body to a campsite at nearby Big Wapomeo Island. Dickson stayed with the body while Rowe paddled to Little Wapomeo and picked up Dr. Howland.

It was July 16, and finally starting to get warm after a cool spring. The body was badly decomposed, so Dr. Howland had it covered with potato sacking but left it in the water alongside the campsite. The water would provide at least some coolness.

Authorities outside the park were notified. A coroner, Dr. A. E. Ranney of North Bay, was called. He would catch a train and arrive at the Canoe Lake Station at eight o'clock that evening. He would conduct an autopsy, and there would be an inquest.

News of Thomson's death shocked the community. It was hard to comprehend that someone so skilled in the woods and on the water could meet such an end.

The two fishing guides stayed with the body as the day moved into evening and toward the eight o'clock train arrival.

The train arrived, but when it pulled away there was no sign of the coroner. The guides built a campfire and kept a gruesome vigil all night. The sun came up hot on July 17, and they were faced with another day of staying beside a body rotting in the shallow water beside the campsite.

## A Body Twice Buried

They and others were upset. It seemed sacrilegious to stand about watching the body of a man everyone knew and respected rot in the July sun. Robinson called Park Superintendent Bartlett and asked permission to bury the body. Bartlett concurred but asked that Dr. Howland examine it and make a report.

Thomson's body was pulled from water and placed on two planks set together. Howland began what was to be a routine examination but immediately made discoveries that have not been explained to this day.

The body was badly swollen and blistered. That was to be expected after nine days of decomposition. However, there was a bruise on the left temple and blood in the right ear. These told the doctor that Thomson had fallen or been struck before entering the water and drowning. Also, there was some air in the lungs.

Just as interesting, fishing line was wrapped around Thomson's left ankle. Some reports said it was tangled line loosely wrapped, but Robinson insisted later it was neatly wrapped, 16 or 17 turns of it, indicating it was placed deliberately.

Two undertakers were called in from towns outside the park. When Dr. Howland finished his examination, they worked on the body to reduce the swelling so it would fit into a coffin. They placed it in an oak coffin, and boated it across to the mainland where it was loaded on a makeshift horse-drawn hearse.

A funeral was hastily thrown together. A small clutch of friends, guides, park staff, and Mowat Lodge guests followed the hearse up the hill roughly one-half a kilometre northwest of the lodge to the cemetery.

There were only two graves there, plus the freshly dug one for Thomson. One contained the remains of Jim Watson of Parry Sound, a young man killed in a mill accident. The other was the resting spot of Alexander Hayhurst, the child who died in the 1915 diphtheria outbreak.

The inscription on the Watson marker provided little comfort for the mourners. It read:

*Remember, comrade, when passing by,*
*As you are now so once was I,*
*As I am now so you will be;*
*Prepare thyself to follow me.*

The little group gathered around the freshly dug hole less than 10 metres behind the two older graves. All the Bletchers were there, with Martin Sr. conducting a brief service of Bible passages. The group, including Hugh Trainor and his wife and Winnie, made its way back down the hill while the undertakers filled the grave.

## A Body Twice Buried

A few hours later, Coroner Ranney appeared on the evening train. The train that brought him took away Winnie Trainor, who decided to leave Canoe Lake immediately after the funeral. Dr. Ranney was picked up and taken to the Bletcher cottage. An inquest was called for 10 p.m. and anyone with knowledge of the death was rounded up.

The inquest was held in the Bletcher's dining room. The only records that remain of that evening are recollections passed on over the years. Dr. Ranney's official report was lost over time. Most of the inquest was devoted to Dr. Howland's examination of the body. Seven persons testified as to what they knew.

Dr. Ranney, who noted he missed his original train because of medical emergencies, ruled Thomson died of accidental drowning and left on the morning train.

This whirlwind of events over less than two days — finding the body, post-mortem exam, inquest, and burial — swirled through Canoe Lake without any involvement of the Thomson family. They were informed of the death by telegram. Shannon Fraser followed that up with a letter to John Thomson on July 18.

*Dear Sir:*

*We found your son floating in Canoe Lake on Monday morning about 9 o'clock in a most dreadful condition the flesh was coming off his hands. I sent for the undertaker and they found him in such a condition he had to be buried at once. He is buried in a little graveyard overlooking Canoe Lake a beautiful spot. The Dr. found a bruise over his eye and thinks he fell and was hurt and this is how the accident happened.*

    *Yours truly*

    *J. S. Fraser*

Dr. Ranney was riding the train back to North Bay on July 18, the morning after the burial and inquest, when Shannon Fraser received a telegram from another undertaker, this one in Huntsville. It said the Thomson family had ordered him to exhume Tom's body and bring it home.

Exhumation is a drastic step, and the order to dig up Thomson's body says something about the feelings of the Thomson family. They must have been upset that the burial was at Canoe Lake rather than at home on Georgian Bay.

They also must have been upset that they were not consulted on the funeral arrangements. Presumably if they had been consulted, the body would have been shipped directly to Owen Sound.

Why they were not consulted is another piece of the puzzle lost in the mists of time. They received a telegram and letter saying what was being done but apparently were not asked about burial arrangements.

Algonquin Park had interior telephone connections as early as 1911, and by 1917 these could be connected to the outside world via North Bay and Orillia. Mark Robinson was able to telephone Superintendent Bartlett at park headquarters, and presumably Bartlett could have called outside the park.

**The Night Visitor**

Tom Thomson had been in his grave just over 24 hours when a man in a black bowler hat and long dark coat stepped from the 8 p.m. train at Canoe Lake Station.

Shannon Fraser was there delivering a trunk for shipment and encountered the man. He learned that he was F. W. Churchill, undertaker from Huntsville. Fraser was surprised to see him because, although he had received his telegram, it had not said when he would arrive.

Churchill explained he had a coffin with him and would need assistance transporting it to the gravesite. The coffin was metal so it could be sealed with solder to prevent the stench of decay from leaking out into the train and upsetting the passengers on the trip to Owen Sound.

Fraser helped load the coffin onto his horse-drawn

wagon and they set off, making a stop at the lodge to pick up a shovel, crowbar, and two lanterns. They continued on to the cemetery, and when the coffin was unloaded Churchill told Fraser to leave and to return at midnight. He said he needed no help for the chilling job at hand.

No one was there to witness Mr. Churchill's work but it must have been a ghoulish scene. Two small lanterns flickering on the hillside overlooking the lake. The silhouette of the bowler hat and bouncing formal coattails. Shovelsful of soil, still loose from being dug out the day before, flying into the darkness at grave's edge. The clunk of the shovel finding the coffin. The screech of the lid being pried open with the crowbar. Then the macabre scene of Churchill pulling the decaying body erect and dragging it up and into the metal box.

Fraser returned three hours later, right around midnight, and found Churchill and the coffin ready to go. They loaded it, and he commented later that the weight distribution seemed wrong. They took the coffin to the station, then returned to the lodge where Churchill spent what was left of the night.

Early the next morning Mark Robinson walked by the station and noticed the coffin and the undertaker waiting for the morning train. He asked what was going on and was told pretty much: Who wants to know?

Robinson showed his ranger's badge, and Churchill told him he was taking the body of Tom Thomson home. Robinson objected, noting that a body could not be removed without approval from authorities. Churchill said the Thomson family orders were the authority he needed.

Robinson reported the situation immediately to Superintendent Bartlett, who said there had been enough trouble over the Thomson death and to let Churchill take the body. Bartlett ordered him to check the gravesite to make sure it had not been left open. He did, and reported that it looked like it had not been fully dug out in the first place.

Railway workers loaded the coffin onto the train, and years later there were rumours that they said it felt too light to contain a man's body. That would be mixed with Fraser's observation about weight distribution to build a theory that Churchill merely shovelled some dirt into the coffin and had not really taken the body.

Part of that theory is based on the strenuous tasks that undertaker Churchill faced alone that dark night in the graveyard. He had to dig the grave, an easier task than usual because it was only a day old, open the coffin, remove the putrid body and wrestle it to the surface, then load it into the shipping coffin. Mark Robinson obviously didn't think all that was possible in three hours.

The coffin was brought to Owen Sound where John and Margaret Thomson lived after moving from the farm. The funeral was held July 21 in Knox United Church. The minister, Rev. P. T. Pilkey, wrote in the death register:

"Talented, and with many friends and no enemies. Mystery."

The coffin was then taken through Owen Sound and along the country road to the cemetery at Leith and placed in the ground in view of the old family farm.

But was there really a body inside? Mark Robinson died an old man, firm in the belief there was not.

As if there were not enough twists in the story, another developed.

Author Roy MacGregor, whose uncle, Roy McCormick married Marie Trainor, wrote in an addendum to his novel *Canoe Lake* of a strange but true meeting in February 1973 in Huntsville's Empire Hotel. Jimmy Stringer, fondly known as the 'mayor' of Canoe Lake and a close friend of Winnie Trainor, told him at the meeting that there were actually three burials — the original at Canoe Lake, one at Leith, and a secret one at another Canoe Lake site.

Stringer said that when Thomson's friends heard an

undertaker was coming to exhume the body, they hastily dug it up themselves and reburied it in another spot at the Canoe Lake Cemetery before undertaker Churchill arrived. He said he had proof and invited MacGregor to come to Canoe Lake when the snow melted and he would show him.

The day after that meeting Jimmy Stringer was crossing the Canoe Lake ice, pulling a toboggan with supplies. MacGregor wrote that the ice gave way and Stringer drowned — almost exactly in the same place that Thomson's body was recovered. With him went the secret that he promised to reveal.

## Chapter 7
# The New Grave Diggers

Controversy over Tom Thomson's death and burials grew stronger with time. It began after the late night inquest at Canoe Lake, and rose and fell like gusts of wind throughout the passing years. With it came talk of ghosts.

Mark Robinson was quoted many times as feeling the inquest left suspicions among the lake people.

"There is considerable adverse comment regarding the way evidence had been taken at the meeting, among residents of the lake," Robinson wrote in his diary on July 18, 1917, the day after the inquest. He did not elaborate.

People presumably felt the inquest was hasty and

did not probe important questions. It simply accepted Dr. Howland's post-mortem report and his view that death was by accidental drowning.

No one questioned the bruise on the temple. Nor did anyone ask how a body stays below the surface nine days in the heat of July? How did the fishing line get wrapped so neatly around the ankle?

Besides having these unanswered questions, Thomson's friends could not accept that an expert canoeist and swimmer could spill his canoe and drown.

The Tom Thomson legend grew in proportion to the increasing numbers of people visiting the park. It became popular to canoe the lake and visit the spots where history had been made: the site where the body was found, the remains of Mowat village, the little cemetery, and a memorial cairn built by Thomson's friends on Hayhurst Point.

Never a summer passed without the mystery being discussed around the campfires at Camp Ahmek for boys and Camp Wapomeo for girls, both established on Canoe Lake not long after Thomson's death.

Thomson's burial and presumed exhumation had been at the rear of the Canoe Lake Cemetery north of the other two graves. Gravestones and old picket fences marked the Watson and Hayhurst graves, which were kept reasonably clear of brush. The bush, however, soon reclaimed Thomson's first grave, and its exact location became a matter of speculation.

Many tried to find the grave over the years. Some even traipsed up the Canoe Lake hillside with shovels, intent on digging to prove once and for all where the famous painter was buried. They figured that solving the burial mystery would help solve the overall mystery of how he died.

The mystery reached a new level of frenzy in the 1930s. In 1935, noted author Blodwen Davies published *A Study of Tom Thomson* in which she raised the possibility that Thomson was murdered. Reports of a phantom canoeist in Algonquin Park were already circulating by then. One famous report came from a Mrs. Northway who was a summer resident on nearby Smoke Lake. She told of paddling with her guide one evening in 1931 when a canoe approached carrying a man wearing a yellow shirt. Her guide steered their canoe toward the lone man to exchange greetings, but then the man and his canoe simply vanished.

Mrs. Northway always was curious about what clothing Thomson was wearing when he died, but no one she asked knew the answer. In fact, he was wearing a yellowish tan shirt.

One of Mrs. Northway's cottage guests that summer was Lawren Harris, Thomson's friend and a member of the Group of Seven. He believed her story because, he said, persons taken unexpectedly continue to haunt the places they loved.

Jimmy Stringer said he had seen the ghost one time while canoeing alone. Another time he was guiding an American who was part of a group. Their canoe fell behind the rest, and somewhere along the route the American began yelling from the bow. When Stringer asked what was the matter, the American said he had seen a ghostly canoe with a lone man up ahead. The man in the ghost canoe shouted that someone had drowned, but then the apparition disappeared. When they reached their destination, Stringer learned that one of the lead canoes, carrying the American's brother, had tipped and the brother had drowned.

Stories of a ghost canoeist persisted. People continued to try to solve the Tom Thomson mystery, but nothing of public consequence happened during the next 20 years. Then in 1956 a group of men led by William T. Little of Brampton, Ontario, hiked up to the Canoe Lake Cemetery with shovels and axes and opened the most gruesome chapter in the Thomson story, if not one of the most bizarre incidents in Canadian history.

Little, a reform school superintendent and later a family court judge, and W. J. Jack Eastaugh had spent many summers at Canoe Lake and were always fascinated by the Tom Thomson mystery. During college years they had worked as counsellors at Camp Ahmek. Little first went to Ahmek in 1930 and worked summers there until 1940.

They were amateur artists and had decided to make a return trip to do some sketching in early October 1956. They set off by canoe from Ahmek and found themselves at Hayhurst Point and the Thomson cairn. Then they moved on to the spot where Mowat Lodge had burned after Thomson's death. It wasn't long before they climbed the hillside where a large birch grew near the old picket fencing around the two old gravestones.

Eastaugh, a school principal, set to work painting the birch. Little kept thinking about the events there 40 years before and left his paints untouched as he daydreamed of the past.

Both men had known Mark Robinson and had heard him talk about the inquest and how he did not believe the body had been taken from Canoe Lake. Robinson had told Little that the painter's grave "was just north of the other two graves."

Little lost his mood for painting and interrupted his friend. They began discussing where the grave might be located. Before they were done, they had made an astounding decision — they would return to dig for the grave.

They rationalized that digging the grave would prove once and for all whether Mark Robinson, who had died the previous year, was right that Thomson's body had never been brought to Owen Sound.

"We thought we might be able to throw a little more light on Thomson's death, and perhaps revive an interest in his painting," Little said in a Canadian Press story after the dig.

If they had any second thoughts about the decision, these were washed away by the excitement of stopping by the Bletcher cottage on the way back. The elder Bletchers had died and Martin Jr. had left Canoe Lake forever the year before. The old two-storey place stood empty and forlorn, shutters covering the windows. Then they stopped at Winnie Trainor's white cottage and peered through the windows and saw a hand-painted set of teacups and saucers that they speculated Thomson painted for Winnie.

Winnie was still alive then and would not have been amused to know that someone was snooping outside her cottage. She continued to use the old cottage and was occasionally seen on the hillside at Thomson's original burial site.

Much about the area had changed. Mowat Lodge,

the old mill, and the hospital building all were gone. Trees had grown up over much of the townsite. The shorelines were spotted with cottages and the boys' and girls' camps. However, the atmosphere was thick with the history of the place, and the two men were still talking about their plan when they returned to Ahmek.

The camp was closed after another busy summer, and the only people around were workers locking down the place for winter and the kitchen staff. Eastaugh and Little had supper with the crew and talked about their plan. Two of the men at supper expressed interest in joining a grave-digging expedition. Frank Braught was a retired schoolteacher from Guelph and well-known cottager on the lake. Leonard 'Gibby' Gibson had lived in the Canoe Lake area much of his life.

The next morning, the four arrived at the cemetery with their digging tools. It was a grey day with steady light rain, which must have given them pause to think over what they were about to do.

Digging up graves just wasn't done, unless for official reasons. Questions about the legality of what they did were raised later. Frank Braught remembered that the group became concerned about legal implications.

"We realized that we were in a serious position," he told an interviewer.

However, they rationalized their expedition by

noting that officially Thomson's body had been removed to Leith. If there was no body at Canoe Lake, they were doing nothing wrong — just digging in the dirt.

They cleared brush at a spot north of the two graves and began digging. Six feet down they found nothing but roots and sandy soil. Not one speck of evidence of a grave.

They selected another spot a few feet away and cleared it. Two men started digging while the other two filled the first hole. Down six feet again and nothing.

Searching for Tom Thomson's grave was starting to look like a bad idea. Eastaugh took a break and wandered off toward a spruce tree just beyond the other two holes. He noticed a depression in the earth. The other men agreed that this spot might be worth a try, but if they dug here and found nothing, they would give up the search.

The digging was difficult near the tree. Roots had to be chopped out, and only one man could work the hole at a time. The hole deepened, and they climbed in and out, taking turns shovelling.

Braught said that at one point he was in the grave head first with the others holding him by the feet.

At the five-foot level, Little took his turn. His shovel hit wood, and he tossed a fragment up to the other men. They said it was a piece of root.

Little recalled later in media interviews:

"We had practically given up our digging. Then I caught hold of what I thought was a small root but it turned out to be a pine plank. This led us to believe we had discovered something."

More shovelling, and more wood appeared. Little realized that one of the pieces of wood was bevelled. It was a piece of a coffin or box used to enclose a coffin. He dug more and broke off a piece of machined wood and brought it to the surface.

Gibson jumped into the hole and began rooting with his hand. He reached into a cavity of what appeared to be the end of a box and pulled out an object that stunned everyone. He held in his hand a piece of human foot bone.

The four men dug out more of the grave, revealing a box caved in on an oak coffin, which also had collapsed through decay and the weight of the earth. The coffin handles were in good shape and there was a plate with the letters "Rest in Peace" but no engraved name. The coffin and outer box matched descriptions from Thomson's funeral: oak coffin with a brass plate and metal handles, plus the softwood box.

The grave revealed little more than the skeleton. There were the remains of what appeared to be coffin cloth or a shroud, but no clothing pieces such as belt buckle, buttons, boots, or other clothing remnants. The men noted that Thomson was buried without his clothing, which had been removed when his body was examined.

The skull later provided interesting evidence. It had been broken in the area of the left temple.

The diggers took a leg bone from the grave and brought it to Dr. Harry Ebbs, a medical doctor staying at his cottage on Little Wapomeo Island. He identified it as the tibia of a man who had stood roughly six feet tall.

Little and companions were convinced: These were the bones of Tom Thomson. They had proven he had not been removed to Leith as many suspected and examination of the bones might show that he had not drowned accidentally, but had been murdered.

They decided it was time to call in the authorities.

# Chapter 8
# The Investigations Begin

On October 5, 1956, more than 39 years after Thomson's death, the Ontario Provincial Police and a crime lab specialist walked up the northwest hillside of Canoe Lake to begin an official investigation.

Corporal A. E. Rodger and Dr. Noble Sharpe carefully emptied the grave, screening and sorting every piece of material. They packed it up and sent it to the provincial crime lab in Toronto.

The men who found the grave and dug up the bones hoped to keep the discovery secret until the investigation was complete. The news media, however, got hold of the OPP report and all hell broke loose.

## The Investigations Begin

One of the two undertakers originally called to Canoe Lake to deal with Thomson's body was outraged. He accused the group of desecrating the Canoe Lake Cemetery, suggesting that in some jurisdictions they would be jailed for disturbing a grave. He asked why, if they were so convinced Thomson's body was at the lake, they didn't get a legal exhumation order to investigate the Leith grave?

In fact, there had been several attempts to settle the mystery by asking the Thomson family to agree to exhumation. The family members insisted the body was at Leith and would never agree. George Thomson, 89, told the media a week after the discovery that he had authorized the move of the body from Canoe Lake to Leith and he was positive it had been done.

F. W. Churchill, the undertaker who opened the Canoe Lake grave that dark night in 1917, got into the fray. The newspapers quoted him as saying Thomson's family and friends were not happy with the burial spot. He said he had received a telephone call from Blodwen Davies, a Thomson friend, and she pleaded with him to exhume the body and take it to Leith.

This only distorted the Thomson story even more. Blodwen Davies in 1917 was a child in Fort William, Ontario, and had never heard of Tom Thomson. Also, Churchill said that when he arrived to do the exhumation, four helpers were supplied by Mark Robinson, who later denied this.

Churchill was entering old age when he made the statements and his memory might have failed him. Some people believe that he mistakenly said Davies had called him when in fact he meant to say Winnifred Trainor.

One interesting thing he did say was that when he removed Thomson's body he placed the empty coffin back into the rough holding box and reburied it.

Media coverage revived the original speculation surrounding Thomson's death and created all sorts of new theories. Dr. Ebbs was convinced a bullet made the hole in the skull. He advanced the theory that Thomson was shot in ambush.

The provincial crime lab began a study of the bones and materials taken from the grave. An anatomy expert was called in.

The investigation didn't take long. On October 19, 1956, the newspapers reported that the crime lab had determined the bones were not those of Thomson. Little and his group were devastated and unwilling to accept the findings.

The crime lab concluded the bones had been buried 20 to 40 years. They belonged to a male roughly five feet, eight inches tall and less than 30 years old. The bones were definitely Mongolian type, meaning they belonged to a Native. The report also noted the three-quarters-of-an-inch hole in the skull and said it likely was a surgical hole made to relieve bleeding following a blow to the head.

Dr. Sharpe said a bullet or a blow from a blunt instrument did not make the hole.

"It is more likely perfectly normal erosion," he said.

All this added more questions to the case. For instance, how did the bones of a Native man end up inside Tom Thomson's original coffin?

There was no question in the minds of the experts that the bones were Native. But no one could explain how they got into the grave. You had to believe that an unknown young Native man was wandering through the area, died, and was buried by friends and/or relatives. At some point, the young man had suffered a blow, which some doctor had operated on. Presumably the injury was acquired some time before death because there were no facilities for surgery anywhere near the burial site.

**Tom Thomson: The Movie**

With one mystery piled upon another it seemed unlikely that anyone now could sort out what really happened back in 1917. Thirteen years passed after the Little group's discovery and the controversy was still hot. The Canadian Broadcasting Corp. decided to take another look at the mystery, airing on February 6, 1969, *Was Tom Thomson Murdered?*

Like every other attempt to solve the mystery, this one raised more unanswered questions.

Dr. Sharpe confirmed during the program his belief that the bones found by the Little group were definitely Native. He said Thomson had very typical Caucasian features. He added that the Native body was buried after Thomson and based this on a piece of wool sock found in the grave.

The sock was the only evidence of clothing in the grave. This confirmed what the Little group had found: The body had been buried naked.

No one could explain why anyone would be buried naked except for one sock. However, Dr. Sharpe said the sock showed the body was buried after Thomson's death because most textiles rotted within five years.

He also offered the opinion that the Native man's body was probably buried on top of Thomson's original coffin.

"He was buried probably naked, except for one sock, in or on top of a coffin which appears to be too expensive for his race."

The CBC program created enough interest that the

matter was raised in the Ontario legislature when Arthur Wishart, attorney general at the time, was pressed to clear up the mystery once and for all.

The exchange was recorded as follows:

Mr. L.A. Braithwaite, member for Etobicoke: "Mr. Speaker, I have a question for the Attorney General: In view of the recent CBC program on the possible murder of Tom Thomson and in view of the many questions raised by that program does the Attorney General wish to make a statement? The second part of the question: Does the Attorney General propose that the grave be re-opened in order to verify that there is a body therein and the skeleton is that of Tom Thomson?"

Hon. Mr. Wishart: "No Mr. Speaker I have no wish to make a statement and I have no intention of making a statement about the CBC program. I certainly have no intention of ordering that the grave be re-opened at all. Perhaps if I were to get a request from some close member of the family, I would consider it, but I would hope that nobody would disturb the situation any more than it has been disturbed."

So there it was left. An unknown young Native man with a hole in his skull had died and was taken to Canoe Lake Cemetery. Someone buried him naked except for one sock. They dug out a grave in the exact spot that Thomson was buried, perhaps even dug up the original coffin and used that.

The situation was so unbelievably bizarre it's no wonder the attorney general's department wanted no further involvement.

There were other attempts to have the Leith grave re-opened. George Thomson, Tom's nephew told the newspapers in 1969 that the family always believed the death was accidental, that the body was at Leith, and that no one ever would allow opening of the Leith grave.

As recently as 1996 there were reports that Thomson descendants were considering granting their permission. Nothing came of that and the family continued to believe that digging the grave would be desecration.

Dr. Sharpe, for all his thoroughness and analysis, seems to have been as puzzled by the case as everyone else.

In an answer to a question for the CBC program he was reported as saying:

"I too think Tom Thomson may still be buried somewhere in the park but I also think we may have opened his original grave and he was not there." Considered more than three decades later, that statement adds to the intrigue. Did Dr. Sharpe mean that he was pretty sure they opened Thomson's original grave but maybe they were wrong? Or, by saying the body still could be in the park, did he know what Jimmy Stringer professed to know and promised to show Roy MacGregor? Was there really a possibility of a third burial?

# Chapter 9
# Solving the Mystery

So many questions. So few answers.

Where is Tom Thomson buried? What happened to his favourite paddle? Who is the Native man in his original grave? How did he get there? What really happened on that weekend in July 1917?

The questions divide into two categories: those surrounding his death; those concerning his burials.

The first question is, what was the hurry to bury Tom Thomson? He was found Monday morning and buried Tuesday afternoon.

It was hot and the body already badly decomposed. No doubt, however, there was an icehouse at Mowat.

## Solving the Mystery

Every bush community had one. It was a necessity for keeping perishables cool. Thomson's body could have been cooled until the coroner finally arrived.

Human nature is a possible answer to why the body was buried without waiting for the coroner. He was supposed to have arrived at 8 p.m. the day the body was found. He didn't and everyone knew he wouldn't for another 24 hours because of the train schedule. These were friends of Tom Thomson, and no doubt they felt the decent thing to do was to bury him without further delay. Letting him float face down in the lake shallows any longer seemed indecent.

More difficult to understand is the lack of consultation with the Thomson family at Owen Sound. George Thomson had been at the lake during the search. He could have come back to claim the body and to witness the delayed inquest. It appears the Thomson family simply was not asked for their views on burial.

George Thomson's exhumation order was tantamount to telling the Canoe Lakers they had done the wrong thing by burying his brother at the lake. That perhaps was the seed from which sprang the controversy and speculation surrounding the burials.

Where Thomson is buried has haunted generations of sleuths trying to solve the mystery. Did Churchill the undertaker do his macabre work in the inky shadows at

Canoe Lake? Or, did he simply sit, smoke a few ciga-rettes, and leave with an empty coffin?

Those who believe Thomson is still at the lake say digging the grave, removing the body, and pulling it out and into another coffin, which had to be sealed, could not have been done in three hours.

On the other hand, the grave was said to be only four feet deep. The earth was sandy and loose, having been dug the day before. Undertakers were used to heavy lifting. Sealing the coffin involved soldering some seams, and soldering can be quick work. Churchill could have had the solder and a small torch in the black bag he is known to have carried.

Churchill, in a 1956 interview in the *Toronto Star*, said he had four men to help with the digging. He said the body was in bad shape but still recognizable. He said Dixon, the original undertaker, had been asked to do the exhumation but refused and that's how he got the job.

The strongest argument that Churchill did do his job is in reports that John Thomson identified his son's body at Owen Sound. John McKeen, a friend and neigh-bour, maintained that he was present when the light metal coffin was brought to the Thomson Fourth Avenue home in Owen Sound. The undertaker said opening the coffin would not be pleasant, but John Thomson insisted. The scene indeed was not pleasant, but Thomson confirmed the body was that of his son.

Tom's sister, Margaret, confirmed the McKeen story. She recalled the coffin being brought into the family parlour. Present were her sister, Elizabeth, brothers, George and Fraser, and McKeen and her father. She said only her father viewed the remains.

It is possible the family told this story to stop once and for all the talk about where the body was buried.

However, it is difficult to imagine any family burying a son or daughter without personally confirming the death. The world is filled with stories of people haunted by being told a loved one was dead, but never knowing for sure. Death is so difficult to accept that visible confirmation becomes mandatory even in the most horrid circumstances.

Does it make sense that John Thomson buried his son without looking into that coffin?

Others will argue just as vigorously that opening the coffin would be repugnant to any family, and most would willingly accept the word of the Canoe Lake witnesses, especially considering that suspicions that undertaker Churchill had not completed the exhumation had yet to be raised.

What makes no sense at all is the skeleton dug up by the Little group. It is difficult to argue that the bones belong to Tom Thomson. Dr. Sharpe's opinion that the bones definitely were aboriginal was confirmed by a noted neuropathologist of the day, Dr. Eric Linnel. Later, Walter Kenyon, an anthropology expert at the Royal Ontario Museum, agreed.

Three experts said the bones belonged to a Native man, and Tom Thomson was not a Native.

When Little's group opened the grave, the coffin and the rough box holding it caved in. Dr. Sharpe's investigation was unable to determine if the skeleton was inside the coffin or had been placed above it. Either way, placing the unknown Native man's body in the precise location of Thomson's first grave is a remarkable coincidence.

Was it possible that someone connected to the Native knew the Thomson story and decided to take advantage of an empty coffin to bury a relative or friend? Or, did someone just pick the spot at random and start digging?

Leonard Gibson said he talked to Winnie Trainor about the 1956 dig, and she said she had given permission to some Natives to bury a body in Tom's coffin. She said the Natives were passing though the area and one died. Few people believed her story.

The identity of the Native is a separate mystery. There were no Native communities close by. It is possible the man was a bush worker connected to the sawmill works that operated on and off in the 1920s and into the 1940s.

He had to have been buried after Thomson in 1917 to be on top of or inside the coffin. Remnants of a decaying wool sock were found with the bones of one foot. Experts said the decaying sock and condition of the bones indicated burial 10 to 20 years previous — between 1936 and 1946.

Perhaps the identity of the skeleton or how it got there does not really matter. What if the experts were wrong and the bones were not those of an aboriginal? What if they are the bones of Tom Thomson?

In the end, the mystery of the cemetery and its bones can do little to solve the overall mystery — how Tom Thomson died. Modern technology might help experts determine if a blow or a surgical procedure or a bullet made the hole in the skull. Or, facial features could be reconstructed from the skull. However, it is unlikely that any modern forensic techniques could prove whether Tom Thomson drowned accidentally or was murdered.

### The Four Possibilities

There are four ways Tom Thomson could have died. He could have taken his own life, had a seizure such as a heart attack or stroke, he could have fallen and hit his head, or he could have been murdered.

The suicide theory was raised soon after Thomson's death. Those who promoted it pointed to Thomson's personality. He had wide mood swings and a violent temper. There was some evidence of depression.

It gained more prominence in 1969 when Charles Plewman, 82, wrote an article in a camping magazine revealing that Shannon Fraser had told him Thomson's death was self-inflicted.

Plewman arrived at Mowat Lodge for a two-month vacation early in July of 1917. He said he was there when the body was found and was a pallbearer at the funeral, although it seems odd that a newcomer who didn't even know the deceased would be given that honour.

He said Fraser indicated that Winnie Trainor was pushing hard for marriage.

"He (Fraser) intimated that she was coming up to see Tom and have a showdown on the fatal week."

Some Thomson friends and acquaintances did not believe that he and Winnie had a heavy-duty romance under way, let alone that they were secretly engaged with marriage planning in the works. They said he was too deeply into his art and the outdoors to fall in love.

"Some say that Tom was too wrapped up in his work to care much for women, and that his bride was the wild mysterious beauty of the northern woods,"

Dr. R. P. Little once wrote.

Others wondered whether his long bachelorhood, moodiness, and tendency to prefer being alone meant that he didn't like women. In fact, he did. He was the typical tall, dark, handsome, and quiet type. Women were attracted to him, and there is no evidence that he shied away from them any more than he stayed away from men at times.

Still the theory that Thomson was being dragged into marriage has some supporting evidence. Daphne Crombie in later years swore that Annie Fraser had seen a letter from Winnie to Thomson saying he 'must' buy a wedding suit. The letter had an urgent tone that suggested a rushed wedding, possibly because of pregnancy.

There seems little doubt that a wedding was planned. The proprietor of Billy Bear Lodge on Bella Lake was reported to have said that Thomson had made reservations for two at the lodge for late in the summer of 1917 and some of his friends had booked rooms as wedding guests.

Terrence McCormick, Marie's son and Winnie's nephew, confirmed that his aunt and Thomson were engaged. Also, a provincial investigator said that Winnie told him in 1956 that she and Thomson had been engaged. As for a possible pregnancy, Winnie's doctor in Huntsville told people over the years that she had never been pregnant.

Whether Thomson was a willing participant in the wedding plans is another story. Some people believed that Winnie was pressing so hard for the marriage that Thomson's only way out was suicide. They combine this with the brooding artist personality, but most followers of the Thomson story consider the theory a bit far-fetched.

Although Daphne Crombie raised the possibility that a rushed wedding was planned, she did not believe the suicide theory. She said in 1977 that Dr. MacCallum approached her after Thomson's death and asked if she believed rumours that Thomson took his own life.

"I said 'utter rubbish.' He (Thomson) was getting all excited about his paintings because they were being recognized. He told me with great big round eyes that he'd just sold one to the government for $500. He was all up in the air about his paintings."

If he wished to escape an unwanted marriage, Thomson had other options. He was a lifelong bachelor, and if he abhorred the thought of marriage, he didn't have to kill himself. He was quite capable of paddling off into the sunset. If there was a pregnancy, suicide would seem an extreme exit. Also, there's only one way to commit suicide in a canoe, and that's to jump out and drown. Thomson's body had a bruise on the left temple and signs of blood in the ear, and surely they would not have been there had he decided to take a deep six over the canoe gunwale.

Thomson's family was outraged by the talk of suicide, and the theory, not strong in the first place, has faded. It created nasty feelings among those attributed to the theory and the family and Winnie Trainor. It no doubt distorted the recollections of those involved.

It's not hard to imagine Thomson having a heart attack and flopping over in his canoe, hitting his head on a gunwale as the canoe tipped. His high cholesterol bush diet that included plenty of eggs and bacon and potatoes, no doubt fried in bacon fat, made him a heart attack candidate. However, he was a trim man who got plenty of exercise and at age 39 was on the young side of the usual heart attack age range. Moreover, there is no evidence of heart disease in the family. Both parents lived long lives for the times and so did his brother George.

More likely is the possibility of an accident. Thomson wouldn't have been the first man to fall out of a canoe while standing and fiddling with his fly buttons.

Friends refused to believe that he could have a canoeing accident. If he did, they couldn't believe he would drown. He was a novice canoeist when he first entered the park but had built experience over several years. He also was said to be an excellent swimmer, having been raised steps from Georgian Bay.

The water that Sunday was warm and calm. Any place he might have fallen in the water along his projected route was within reach of one shore or another for a good swimmer. His route would take him near the lake's western shore and past the islands that separate the south and north ends of the lake.

Consider, however, that a light rain made the interior of his canoe wet and slick. Add to that the likely hangover from the Saturday night party. The carousing and arguing lasted until at least midnight, likely longer. Thomson was known to drink heavily when he was in the mood and had the opportunity. The argument indicates he took on a fair load of alcohol during the evening.

If he had been an aircraft pilot instead of a canoeist that day, Thomson would have been considered unfit to fly early Sunday afternoon. Hangovers are considered worse than light levels of drunkenness for some functions.

Never mentioned in any stories of Thomson's death are the effects flies might have had that day. Anyone who has canoed and fished in blackfly and mosquito season knows the distractions that these nuisances can cause. By his own account, the flies were the worst Thomson had ever seen in the park.

He complained about the flies in the last letter he wrote. He tells Dr. MacCallum in the letter, written the day before his death: "The weather has been wet and cold all spring and the flies and mosquitoes much worse than I have seen them any year and fly dope doesn't have any affect on them."

The bruise on the left temple is an excellent match in a scenario in which Thomson stood to take a leak, slipped and fell, striking his head and tipping the canoe. The annoyance of flies could have been a factor in that, or other accident scenarios.

## Murder, They Wrote

If only it was possible to assemble in one room all the persons who over the years have probed the Tom Thomson mystery. The majority, if asked to vote on how they thought Thomson died, would pick murder. That's the only point on which you would get consensus. Asked to support their conclusions, the group would sink into a miasma of conflicting facts, contradictions, rumours, and half-baked thoughts.

People who believe Thomson was murdered rest their cases on two critical pieces of physical evidence: the bruise on the left temple and the fishing line wrapped around the ankle. They combine that with the stories of arguments between Thomson and Bletcher, or Thomson and Fraser.

Mark Robinson told the story of the fishing line many times. Thomson's body was pulled up on Big Wapomeo Island and laid out for Dr. Howland to examine. Howland, one of the undertakers, and Robinson were present and they began to remove Thomson's clothing. The undertaker noted the wrapping of line and asked Robinson to remove it. Robinson recalls being asked to cut "those strings." He said the line was neatly wrapped 16 or 17 times around the left ankle.

It was common years ago to fish for summer lake trout with copper line. Trout like cool water and as the surface of a lake warms in summer, they move deeper. Weighted line helps to get the lure down to them.

Thomson is known to have used copper line. His homemade reel with a piece of copper line still attached is displayed at the Tom Thomson Memorial Gallery in Owen Sound.

It has always been assumed that the line wrapped on Thomson's ankle was copper. One writer offered the opinion that Thomson might have had a sprained ankle and wrapped it with copper line to hold it stiff.

Robinson insisted the line — he never actually described it as copper — was carefully wrapped, not a loose tangle. The implication was that it had been done deliberately. The most likely reason to wrap the line deliberately was to hold a rock or anchor a murderer might use to weigh down the body.

String and copper are so different it is difficult to believe the undertaker would look at copper wrappings and refer to them as "those strings." String is the term one would use for fabric fishing line.

The difference is important. Copper line simply could not become so neatly wrapped on its own. It is too stiff to be worked neatly by underwater currents. Fabric line could become reasonably neatly wrapped without the help of human hands. Still, it is hard to imagine water currents wrapping any line so neatly as Robinson described.

Jack Wilkinson, an Algonquin Park resident at the time of the tragedy, presented an interesting theory when interviewed by park staff for an oral history project in 1976. His version of the finding of Thomson's body was completely different.

He said that Dr. Howland was fishing with his young daughter when they snagged something. Reeling in, Howland suspected the snagged bundle was a body and immediately left it and took the girl to shore. He returned and towed the body to Wapomeo Island.

Wilkinson claimed it was common practice in drownings to leave a body in the water while officials were summoned. It was also common to tie the body so it would not drift away. He believed Howland wrapped fishing line around Thomson's ankle when he towed the corpse to shore and secured it. He said the line must have been fabric because it is unlikely Howland would use heavy-duty copper line for a child's fishing excursion. This jibes with the undertaker's reference to "those strings."

Mark Robinson no doubt would scoff at this. He was convinced Thomson was murdered and the fishing line was attached to the ankle and an anchor to hold the body at the bottom of the lake. However, nowhere did he record the type of line he removed from the ankle. He did not mention the line until many years after the incident.

The fact that Thomson's body apparently took nine days to surface is seen as odd. It was rotting rapidly, with skin beginning to fall away. Decomposing bodies produce gases that begin to float the body. It is reasonable to ask why it took so long for the body to surface if it had not been anchored.

Dr. Howland wrote in his report of the examination that the only mark on Thomson's body was a bruise, roughly 10 centimeters long on the left temple. There was "some bleeding from right ear" and air escaped from the lungs.

Amateur sleuths have jumped all over this information throughout the decades. They say that dead people don't bruise or bleed, so Thomson must have been struck a blow to his head before entering the water. They also say people who drown have water in their lungs, not air. Experts have said that in a small percentage of drownings, some air does remain in the lungs.

This physical evidence certainly points to Thomson receiving a blow to the head and entering the water unconscious. Much was made of the fact by some people that the hole in the Canoe Lake Cemetery skull is on the left side.

Somewhere throughout the history Mark Robinson was reported to have contradicted Dr. Howland by saying the bruise was on the right temple. However, his diary entry for July 17 notes the wound was on the left temple.

The diary raises no suspicions of foul play. Robinson said the bruise was "evidently caused by falling on a rock." The only diary reference to anything being amiss in the Thomson case is a July 18 notation that there was "considerable adverse comment" about the way evidence was taken at the hasty inquest. Yet those three words alone are a powerful mystery. Why was there adverse comment and what exactly was it?

Many of Robinson's recollections were made long after the event and can be questioned because of the passage of time. But those three words were written the morning after the burial and inquest, and they continue to haunt everyone who researches the story.

## The Suspects

If Tom Thomson was murdered, who did it?

Over the decades fingers have pointed to Martin Bletcher Jr., mainly because he was not well liked at the lake. He was said to be opinionated, obstreperous, and difficult to get along with. He was considered a draft dodger, which he wasn't. He worked for a private detective agency in Buffalo, which some people saw as sleazy work.

Much of the case against Bletcher rests on the Saturday night party and Bletcher's reported warning to Thomson not to get in his way. That combined with the talk that Bletcher was interested in Winnie Trainor is used to build a motive.

However, there is no evidence of any relationship between the two neighbours. Bletcher was 26 at the time, a good eight years younger than Winnie.

Ralph Bice once strongly expressed his take on the love triangle theory:

"The fact that they (Bletcher and Thomson) quarrelled over Winnifred Trainor, that is the most ridiculous slander because Martin Bletcher had a wife who was much, much prettier than Winnifred Trainor."

A more likely theory is that Bletcher's younger sister, Bessie, had eyes for the tall, dark, and woodsy Thomson, and Martin didn't like that. Bessie was single and interested in painting.

The actions of the Bletchers the day of Thomson's disappearance are suspect. Martin and Bessie went down to the lake after Thomson paddled away to go fishing. They headed in the same direction. On their return later in the afternoon they spotted the overturned canoe drifting.

It is hard to imagine anyone seeing an overturned canoe and not raising an alarm or at least checking it out. Martin Bletcher was said to have told the inquest he hadn't taken much note of the canoe because he thought it was one reported to have drifted away from a lodge or cottage.

Why not recover the canoe? One version of the story says he did. Another says the canoe was not brought in until Bletcher mentioned it casually the next day.

Some people tried to build the case that Bletcher, still enraged from the Saturday night argument, followed Thomson down the lake. The argument resumed on the lake or on a portage and Thomson never returned.

However, why would Bletcher mention seeing the overturned canoe at all?

One summer resident of the lake suggested that someone hid in the Bletcher boathouse with a rifle and watched Thomson depart in the canoe. That person then shot him as he paddled down the lake. That would account for the hole in the skull found in Thomson's original grave.

Dr. Sharpe, however, said that aside from the skull not being Thomson's, the hole was not made by a bullet. Also, he sifted the entire grave and did not find a bullet. If a bullet had entered the skull and there was no exit hole, the bullet had to remain in the skull or somewhere in the grave.

A bullet fired from the Bletcher boathouse would have struck Thomson in the right side of the head. Dr. Howland noted the wound was on the left side.

The second suspect in the murder theory is Thomson's friend, lodge owner Shannon Fraser. Thomson had loaned Fraser $200, a significant amount in those days, and wanted it back for his upcoming marriage to Winnie. The loan was to buy canoes for the lodge.

As the Saturday night drinking party broke up and people drifted away, Thomson and Fraser argued about the money. There was a pushing match and Thomson fell, hitting his head at the temple area. He later died and Fraser, panicked by the situation, disposed of the body down the lake.

Winnie Trainor wrote after Thomson's death that the loan had been made in 1915 but Fraser had paid most of it back.

The Fraser theory can be questioned by the fact that Robinson reported having seen Thomson fishing at Joe Lake dam the morning after the party. And of course there is the recollection that Thomson breakfasted with guests at the lodge and later got lunch supplies from Fraser. Some argue that these recollections all trace back to Fraser and there is no direct evidence that Robinson or anyone else except Fraser reported seeing Thomson that Sunday morning.

The Frasers appeared to be good friends of Thomson. They spent much time together, Thomson helping out at the lodge, the Frasers no doubt giving Thomson breaks on accommodation. It almost seems to have been a family relationship.

That changed immediately after Thomson's death. There were harsh letter exchanges between Fraser and Thomson's family. Winnie Trainor, in a letter, made arcane references to tensions at Canoe Lake, particularly involving the Frasers and described them in unflattering terms.

The Frasers were known to have started the suicide theory, saying Thomson could not face the marriage to

Trainor. The suicide rumours enraged the Thomson family and obviously Winnie Trainor. That would have been enough to quickly rip apart the best relationships.

There is a third possibility in the murder theory not involving any of the people at Canoe Lake. It might be called far-fetched but perhaps no more so than some of the assumptions made in the Thomson mystery.

Not everyone welcomed the arrival of conservation thinking at the start of the 1900s. Hunting, trapping, and fishing for big city markets was career work for those who could withstand the elements and the long, hard hours of catching game and preparing it for shipment. Also, many people still depended on catching their own country food. The establishment of preserves and parks and increasing controls on wildlife harvesting cut into the incomes and way of life of some country people.

The response of those who refused to accept the changes was to ignore the law and become poachers. When the railways entered the park, rangers like Mark Robinson met the trains and checked out suspicious passengers who might be sneaking in guns or traps. Thomson himself was checked by Robinson as a potential poacher on one of his early arrivals.

Thomson had worked as a fire ranger and guide and was well aware of the poaching problem in the park. His personality, combined with his love for the wilds, indicates that poaching would be something he could not tolerate.

Is it possible that Thomson saw something illegal on Canoe Lake that day, or on a portage into one of the nearby lakes? Did he encounter someone breaking the wildlife laws and step in? He wouldn't have been the first person murdered by poachers, who were ruthless at concealing their illegalities. Poachers killed three of the first wildlife wardens hired by the Audubon Society to protect U.S. bird nesting sites in 1900. The poaching wars took other lives after that.

Poaching in Algonquin Park was so rampant that some park employees, tempted by quick dollars, were involved. There were documented cases of rangers involved in the illegal fur trade being caught and fired.

An early recounting of the Thomson tragedy had the canoe being found right side up, both paddles lashed in the portaging position. Thomson's lunch was still in the bow but his fishing gear and packsack were missing. It appeared Thomson had beached the canoe and prepared for portaging.

If he did meet his killer on land, his pack and fishing gear were taken away and his canoe set adrift after his body was dumped in the water.

Certainly the theory of death on land is supported by the concentration of the searchers on the bush country and not the lake itself.

There was always much talk of Thomson's favourite paddle being missing. This doesn't jibe with the report that both paddles were lashed in portaging position. Unless of course Thomson kept two paddles permanently lashed for portaging and a third paddle free to work with. This was a known practice among people who did considerable portaging.

## Chapter 10
# A Story without an Ending

People sometimes joke that they hate to see facts get in the way of a good story. The Tom Thomson mystery is a good story, but the "facts" continually send it off in different directions.

Facts are delicate critters. They are play putty, easily shaped by time, misconceptions, and individual perceptions. Depending on what accounts you read, Thomson's favourite paddle was ash or cherry. Winnie Trainor was born in 1882 or 1884. The line wrapped around Thomson's ankle was string or copper fishing line. Undertaker Churchill had four men to help him exhume Thomson's body or did the job by himself. The canoe was found overturned. The canoe was really right side up. A paddle was missing. Both paddles were lashed in portaging position.

Time is a great enemy of facts. It has been 86 years since Thomson's death, and everyone who was part of it in 1917 is gone. Even some of their recollections, made long ago and sometimes long after the incident, are contaminated by the passage of time.

More than time is at work to mask the true facts. The Tom Thomson mystery is so powerful that people who enter it find it impossible to remain neutral. Even if we could go back to July 1917 it would be difficult to find the truth. Those involved were shocked and emotional.

Perhaps it is better that we can't know all the facts. One of the joys of the Tom Thomson story is just the telling and speculating about what really did happen. In some ways it doesn't really matter that we don't know exactly what happened back in 1917. We already know what we need to know:

• Tom Thomson was a Canadian farm kid who like many of us grew through young adulthood wondering what to do in life. He stopped wondering when he started painting seriously.

• He loved the outdoors and was a skilled forest traveller. As an angler, he was devoted and expert.

• He painted the Canadian landscape as he saw it,

not as how the Europeans saw it. The Europeans saw a wild country that needed to be tamed. Thomson saw a raw beauty that needed to be preserved.

• His painting left us a vision of what our country is.

• He died in the wilderness he loved. It doesn't really matter how. It is enough to say he died too soon.

• His bones lie somewhere beneath the Canadian landscape that he loved. It doesn't matter where. His spirit is at Leith, at Canoe Lake, and every place that his paintings hang and where people speak his name.

# Epilogue

It was a long time before any of Tom Thomson's painter friends returned to Algonquin Park to sketch. Some never returned at all. They felt the North Country was not the same following his death.

A group did come back briefly in September 1917. They had rocks hauled up the hill at Hayhurst Point where friend and fellow artist J. W. Beatty mortared them into a cairn. Shannon Fraser and George Rowe helped with the project, financed by Dr. MacCallum. J. E. H. MacDonald designed a bronze plaque that was attached to the cairn face. The plaque reads:

*To the memory of Tom Thomson artist woodsman and guide who was drowned in Canoe Lake, July 8th 1917. He lived humbly but passionately with the wild. It made him brother to all untamed things of nature. It drew him apart and revealed itself wonderfully to him. It sent him out from the woods only to show these revelations through his art. And it took him to itself at last.*

The cairn still stands among the red pines high

*Epilogue*

above Thomson's favourite camping spot.

Thomson's friends moved on, some forming the Group of Seven, the first and most famous Canadian art movement. Although Thomson was gone before the group formed, its members were influenced by his work just as he was by theirs.

His style was seen as highly individual with expressive brush strokes and the use of bold colour that reflected the northern landscape — the outdoors as Canadians know it.

A. Y. Jackson once summed up Thomson's art:

"He gives us the fleeting moment, the mood, the haunting memory of things he felt. Not knowing all the conventions about what is paintable, he found it all paintable; muskeg, burnt trees, drowned land, log chutes, beaver dams, northern lights, flights of wild geese."

Thomson's art became more popular as the decades passed. Owen Sound erected its Tom Thomson Memorial Gallery. The McMichael Gallery obtained some Thomson work and what was left of his shack, erecting it on its property just north of Toronto.

In 2002, to coincide with the 125th anniversary of Tom Thomson's birth, the most extensive exhibition of Thomson's work opened at the National Gallery, and then toured the country.

The year 2003 brought a major revival of interest in Tom Thomson. In May, a lost Thomson work — *Boathouse/Go Home Bay* — re-appeared and was sold at auction for $194,500 including commission and tax. It was painted in 1914 during Thomson's visit to Dr. MacCallum's cottage.

At Huntsville, Thomson soon will sit painting in the downtown civic square in the form of a life-size bronze. Muskoka sculptor Brenda Wainman Goulet has begun work on the piece that has Thomson sitting on a rock beneath a pine tree while he paints the *West Wind*. The sculpture is expected to be unveiled in the fall of 2004.

Perhaps the greatest tribute to Thomson is a simple quote from a man who met Thomson in 1914 in the Georgian Bay area and spent some time with him. Ernest Feure of Guelph wrote in a letter:

"I have seen beauty in the bare and broken branches of trees ever since."

The author at Tom Thomson's cairn

# About the Author

Jim Poling Sr. is the author of two histories on outdoors themes — *The Canoe: An Illustrated History* (Key Porter 2000) and *The Decoy* (Key Porter 2001). In 2003 he published his first collection of short stories titled *Lights in Dark Forests*. He is a frequent contributor to *Cottage Life* magazine. He lives in Alliston, Ontario, but spends much of his time at his cottage not far from the Algonquin Park west boundary. He is the retired general manager and editor of The Canadian Press news agency.

# Bibliography

Addison, Ottelyn. *Tom Thomson. The Algonquin Years.* McGraw-Hill Ryerson, 1969.

Art Gallery of Ontario/National Gallery of Canada. *Tom Thomson.* 2002

Davies, Blodwen. *A Study of Tom Thomson.* Ryerson, 1935.

Little, William T. *The Tom Thomson Mystery.* McGraw-Hill Ryerson, 1970.

MacGregor, Roy. *Canoe Lake (Shorelines).* McClelland and Stewart, 1980.

Miller, Audrey Saunders. *Algonquin Story.* Friends of Algonquin Park. 1946, 1963, 1998.

Shaw, S. Bernard. *Canoe Lake, Algonquin Park.* General Store Publishing, 1996

# Bibliography

Silcox, David P. *Tom Thomson. An Introduction to His Life and Art.* Firefly Books, 2002.

Town, Harold/Silcox, David P. *Tom Thomson. The Silence and the Storm.* McClelland and Stewart, 1977.

# Photograph Credits

# Acknowledgments

No book is produced without much help from other people. The author thanks the following:

Ron Poling, chief of the Photo Service for The Canadian Press, for yeoman's service in the canoe bow on Canoe Lake. And for his excellent photography at the lake.

Brian Bissell, a cottage neighbour on St. Nora Lake, for helping me understand the Algonquin Park region topography in his floatplane C-GBIZ and with computer mapping programs.

Asma Khan, librarian at Canadian Press Toronto, for locating ancient Tom Thomson files for my research.

Erin Collins at the Algonquin Park Archives for digging out material related to Thomson, and some helpful photographs.

Julian Smith, curator of the Billy Bishop Heritage Museum in Owen Sound, for providing help on the war ace's movements in 1917.

My wife, Diane, who never complains about the inordinate amount of time I spend looking into other people's lives and sometimes not spending enough time on our own.

AMAZING STORIES™

## EDWIN ALONZO BOYD

The Life and Crimes of Canada's
Master Bank Robber

HISTORY/BIOGRAPHY
by Nate Hendley

Edwin Alonzo Boyd
ISBN 1-55153-968-3

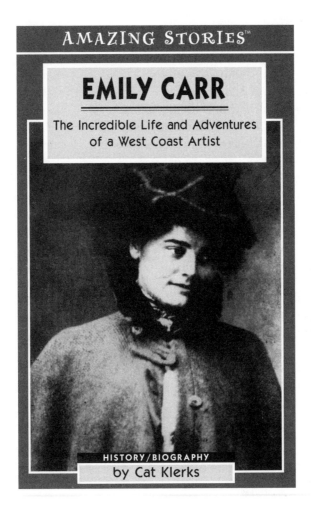

AMAZING STORIES™

# EMILY CARR

The Incredible Life and Adventures
of a West Coast Artist

HISTORY/BIOGRAPHY
by Cat Klerks

Emily Carr
ISBN 1-55153-996-9

## OTHER AMAZING STORIES

These titles are available wherever you buy books. If you have trouble finding the book you want, call the Altitude order desk at 1-800-957-6888, e-mail your request to: orderdesk@altitudepublishing.com or visit our Web site at www.amazingstories.ca

All titles retail for $9.95 Cdn or $7.95 US. (Prices subject to change.)

New AMAZING STORIES titles are published every month. If you would like more information, e-mail your name and mailing address to: amazingstories@altitudepublishing.com.